DANIELA COMANI

SUNSETS

EDITION PATRICK FREY N° 217

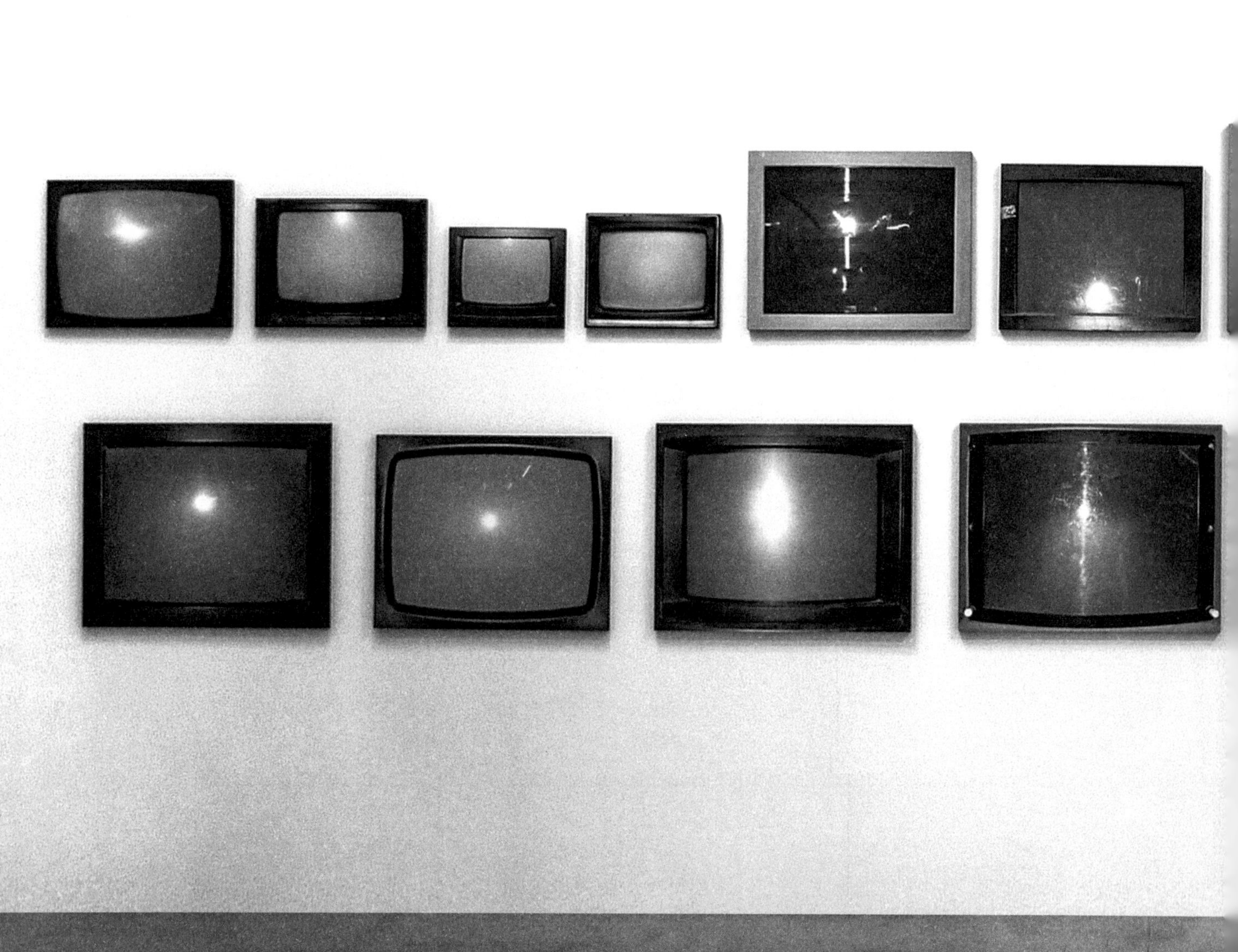

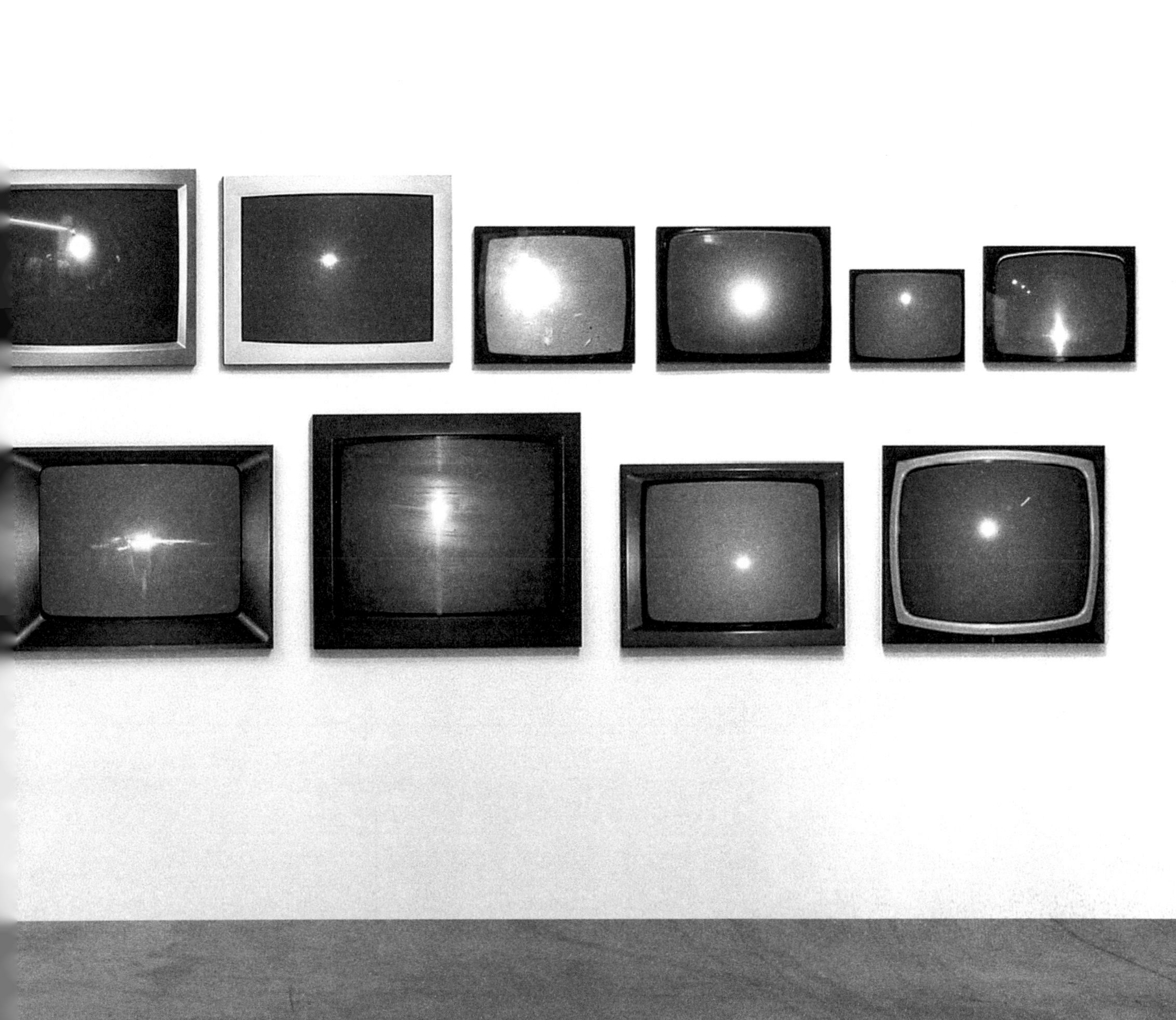

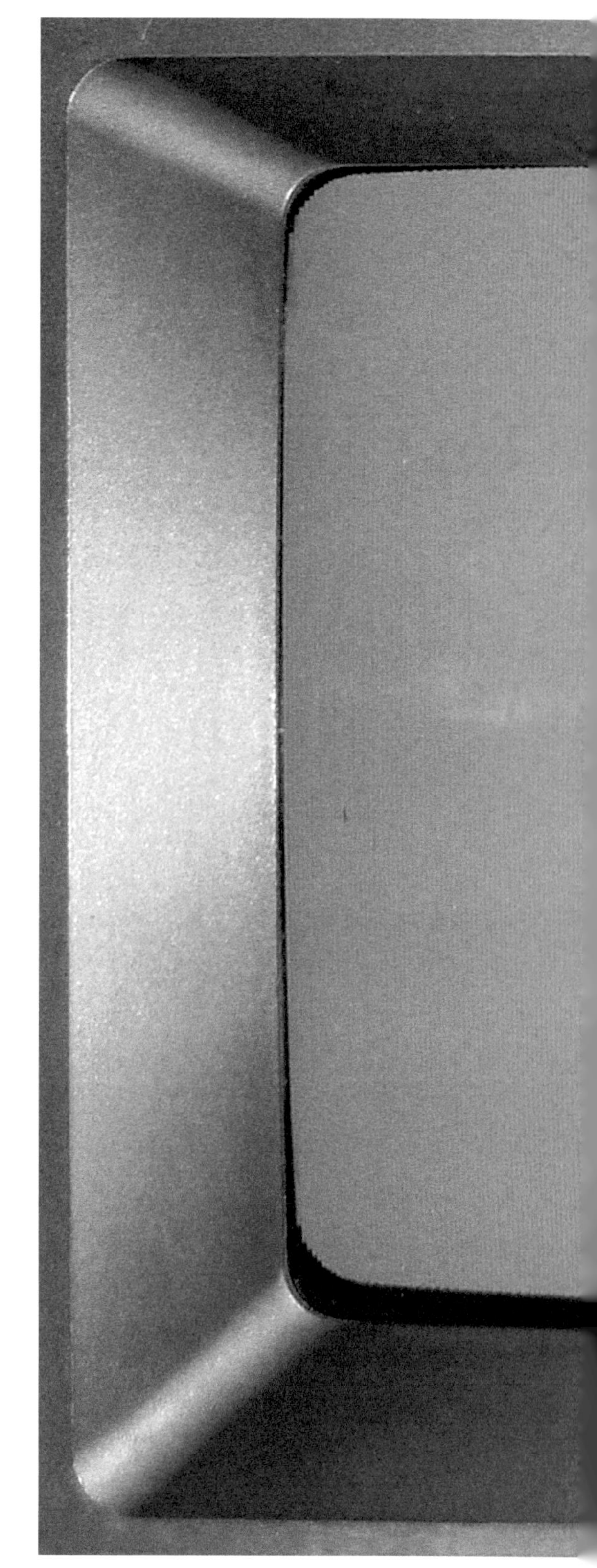

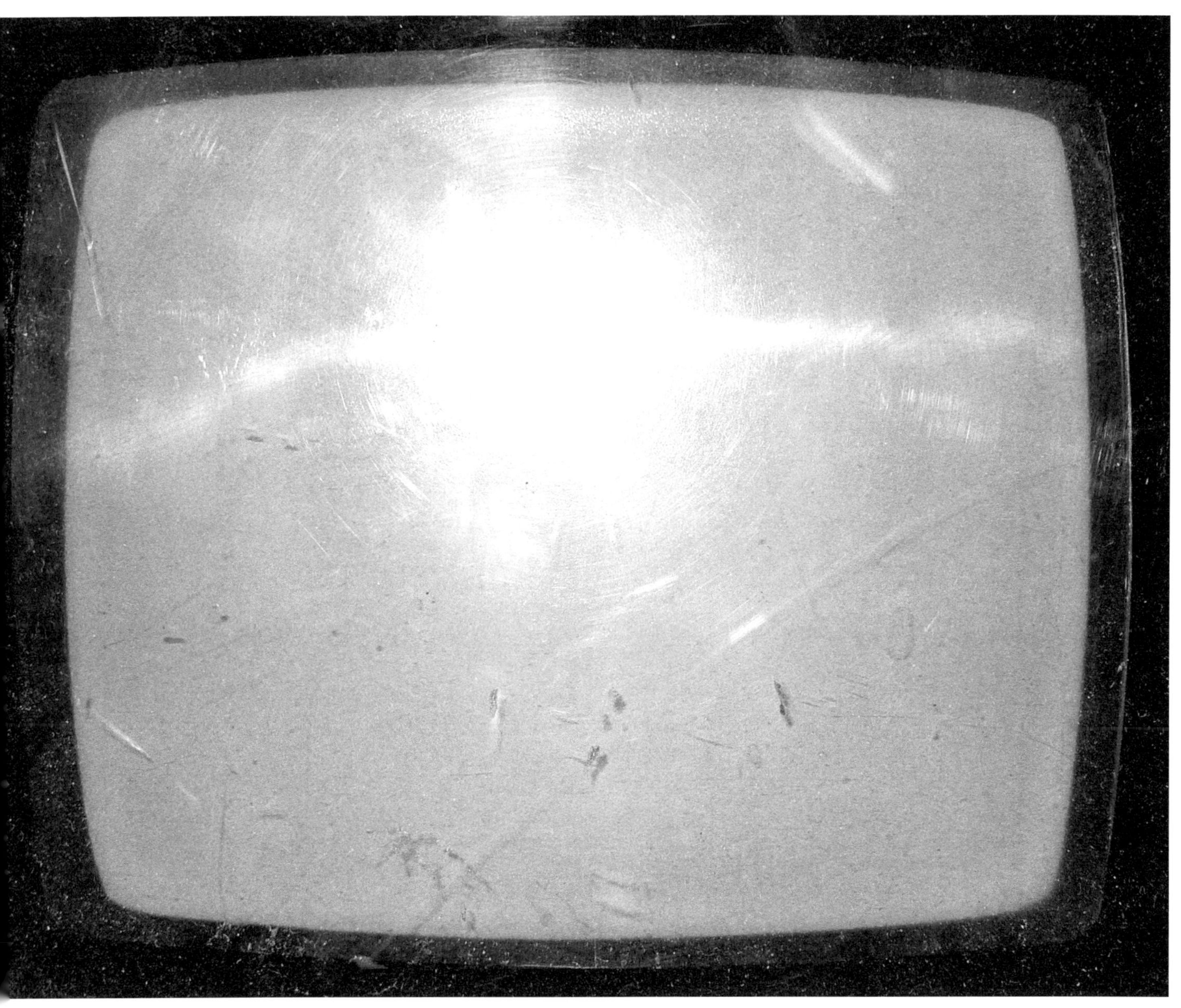

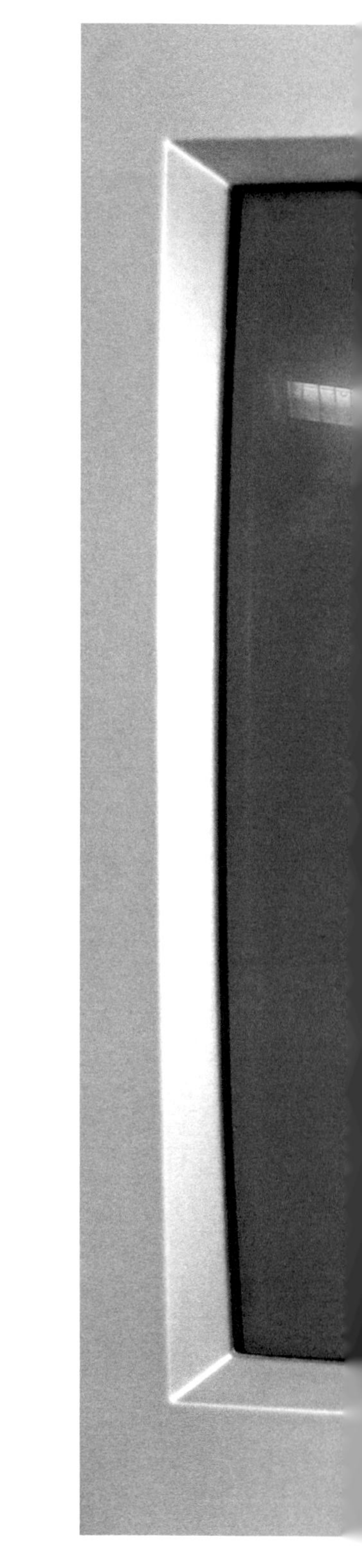

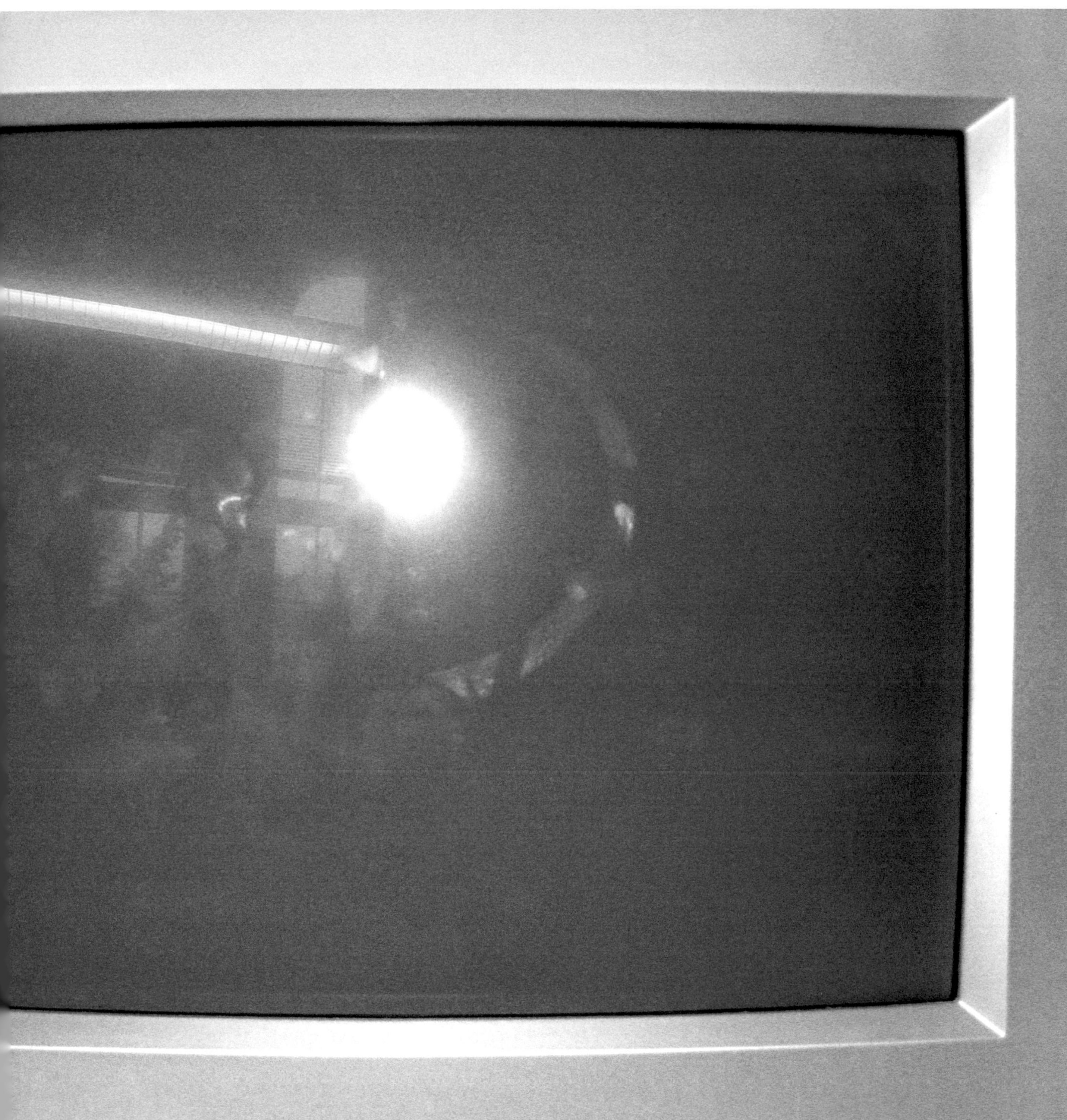

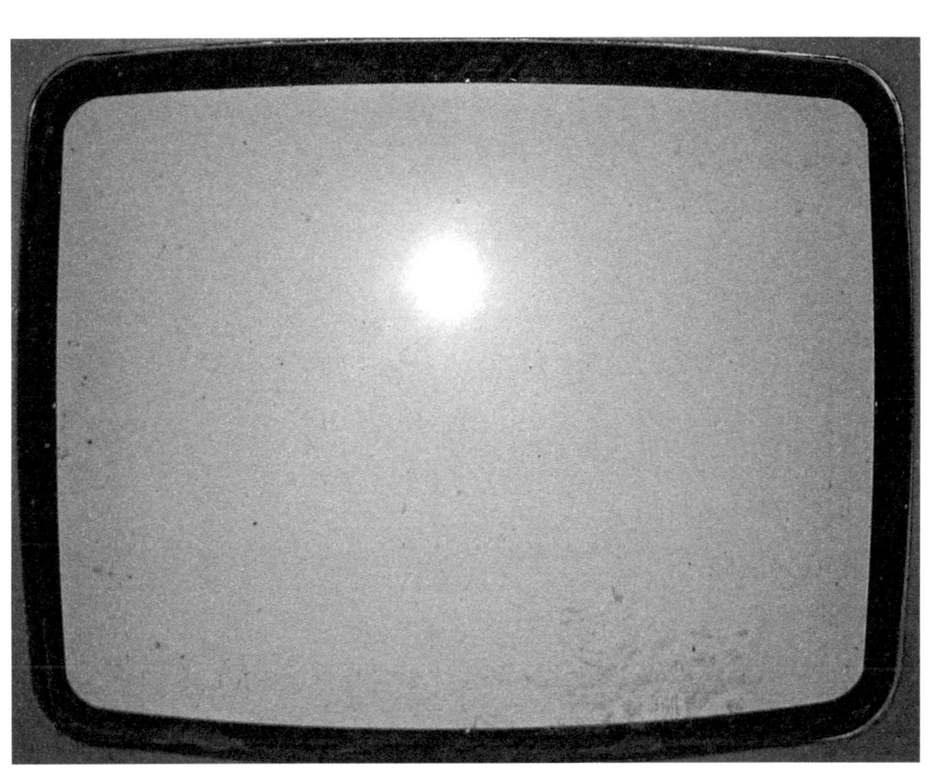

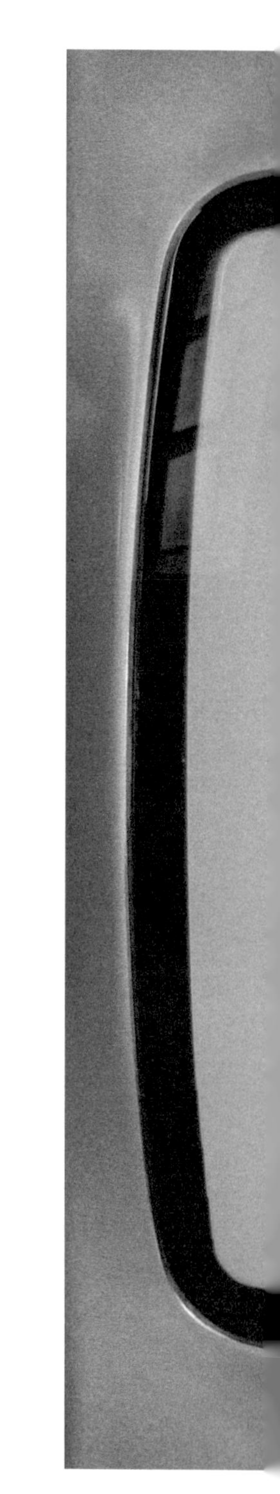

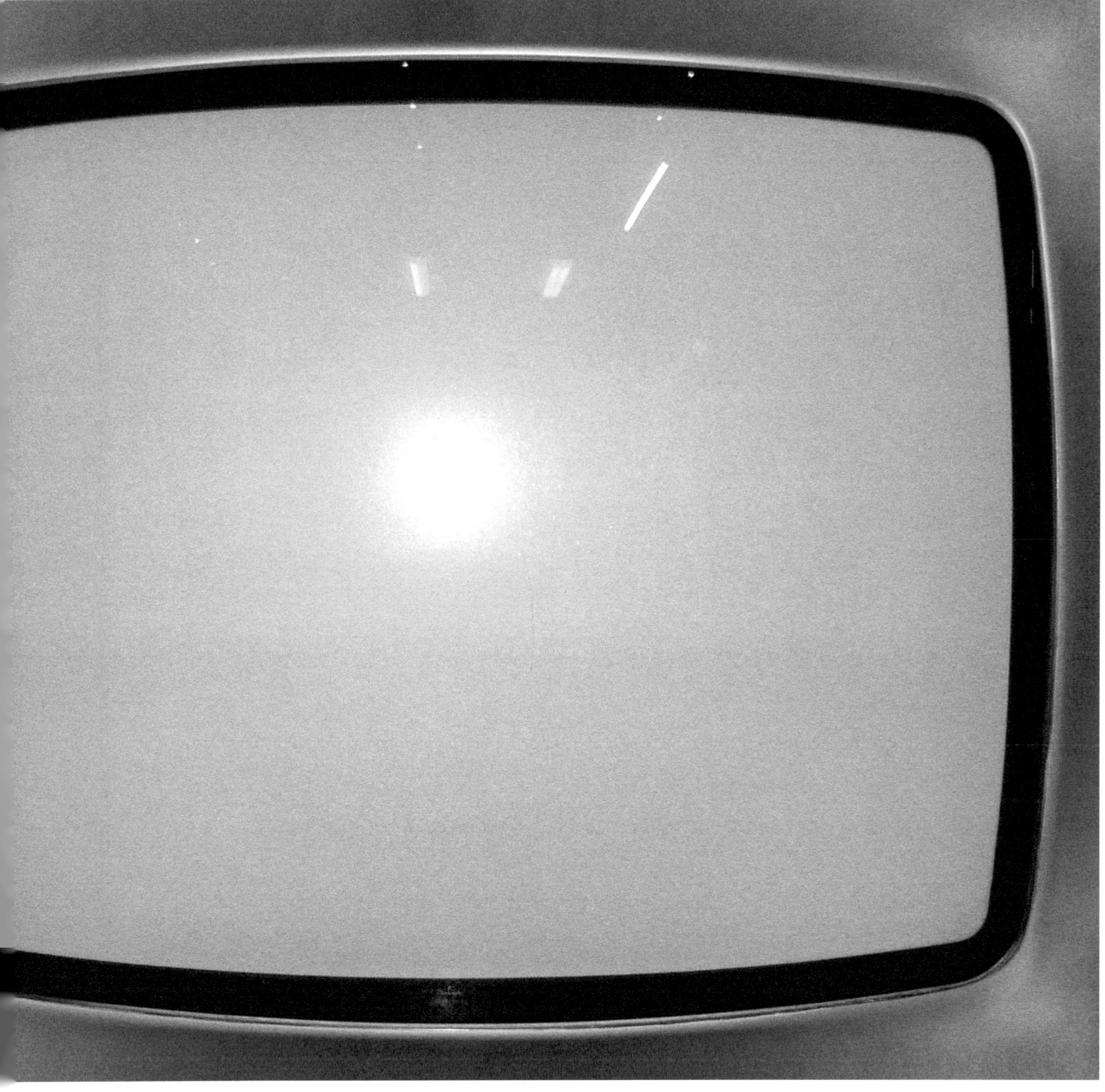

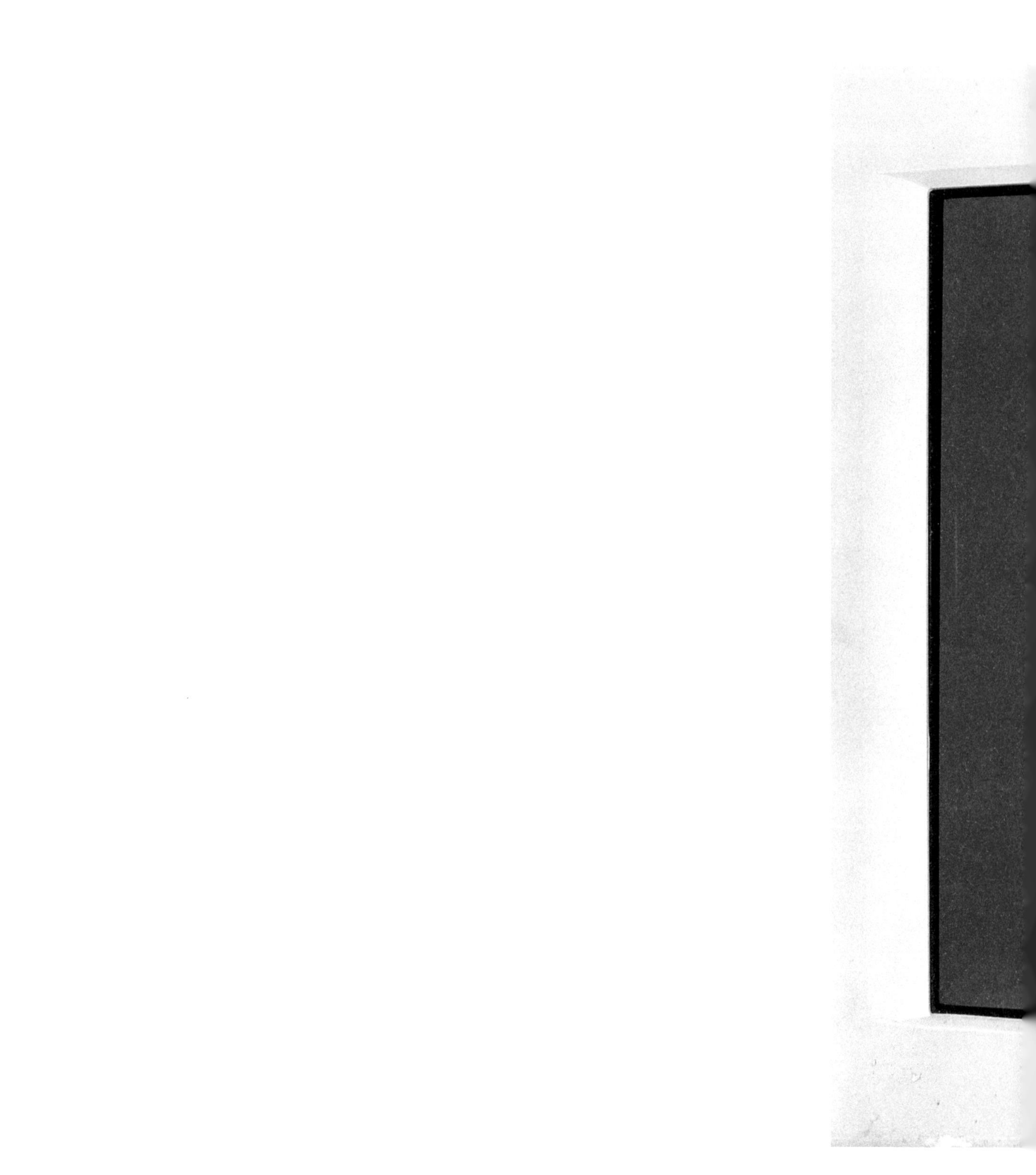

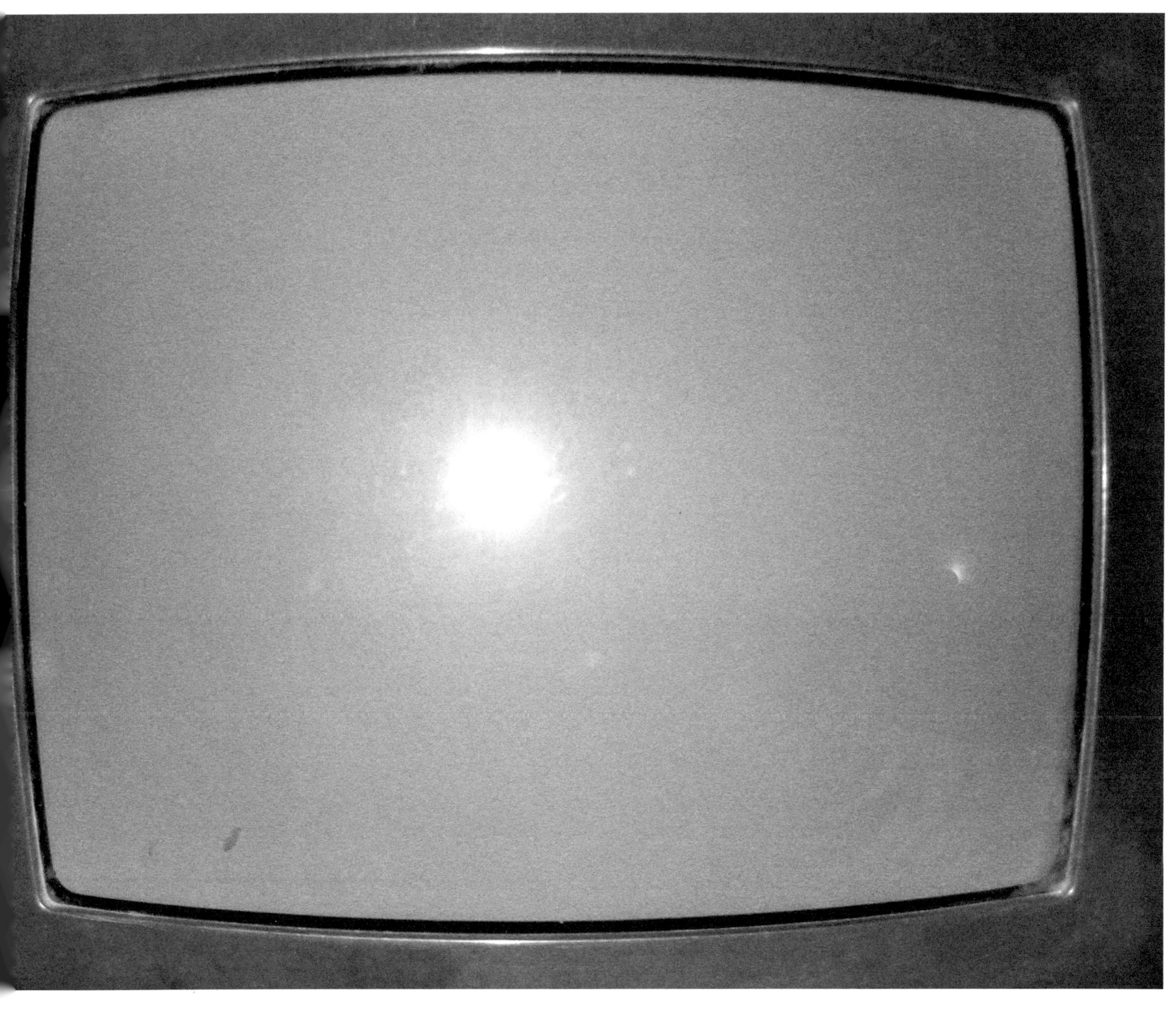

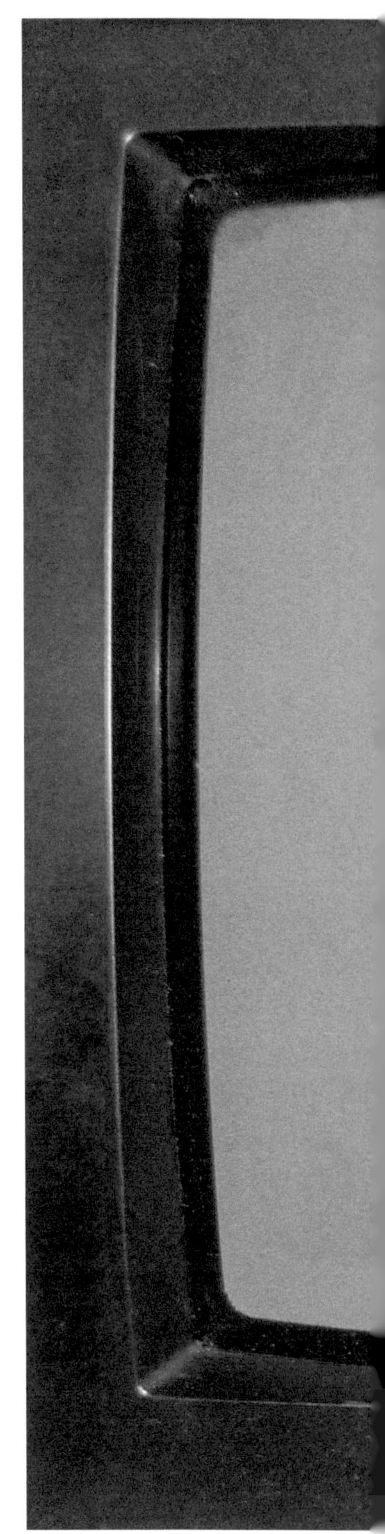

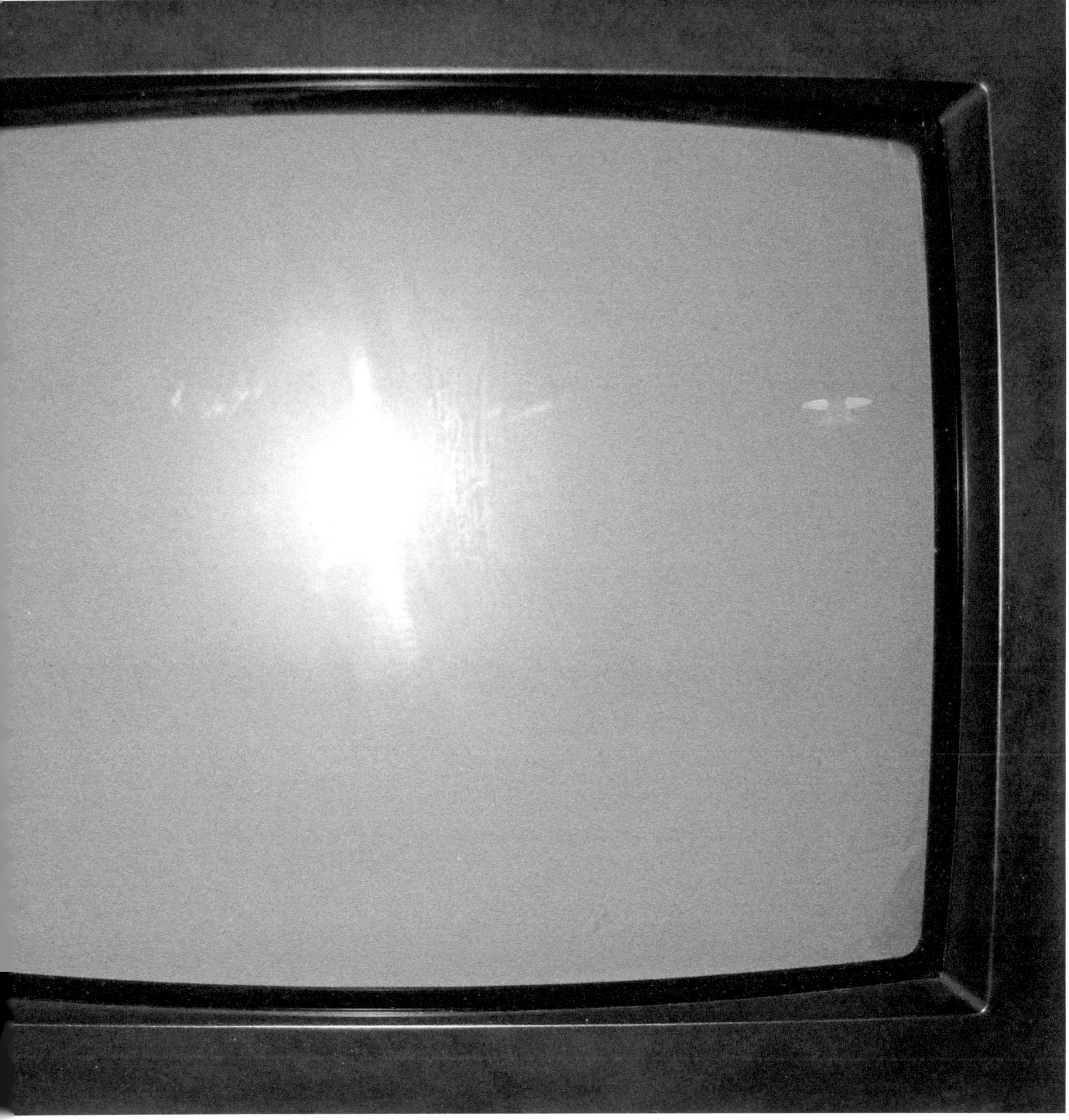

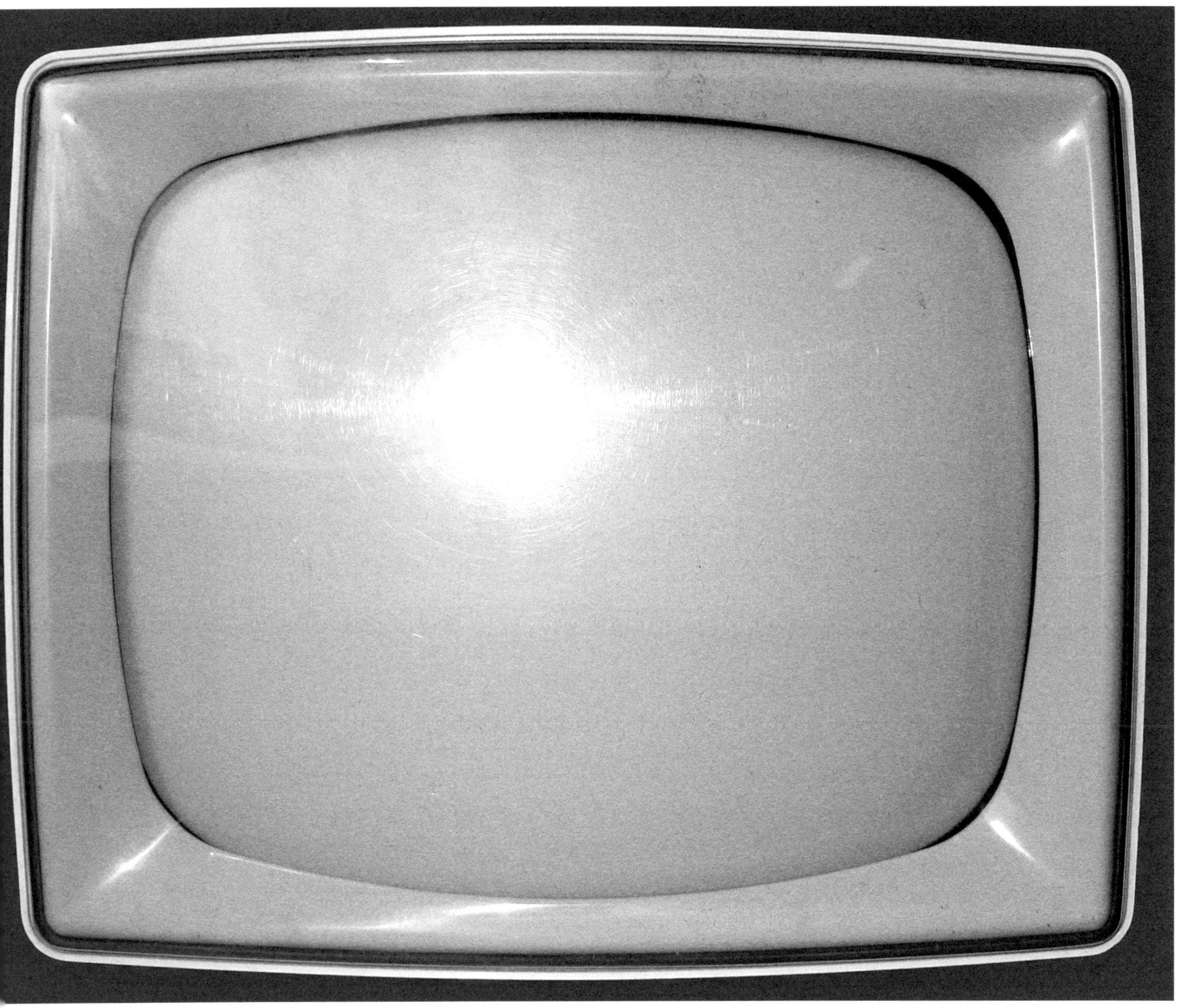

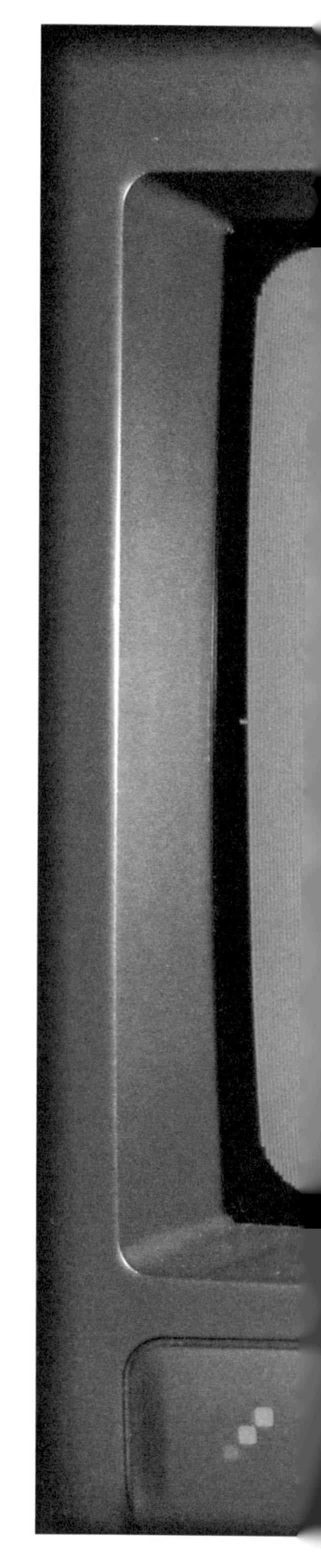

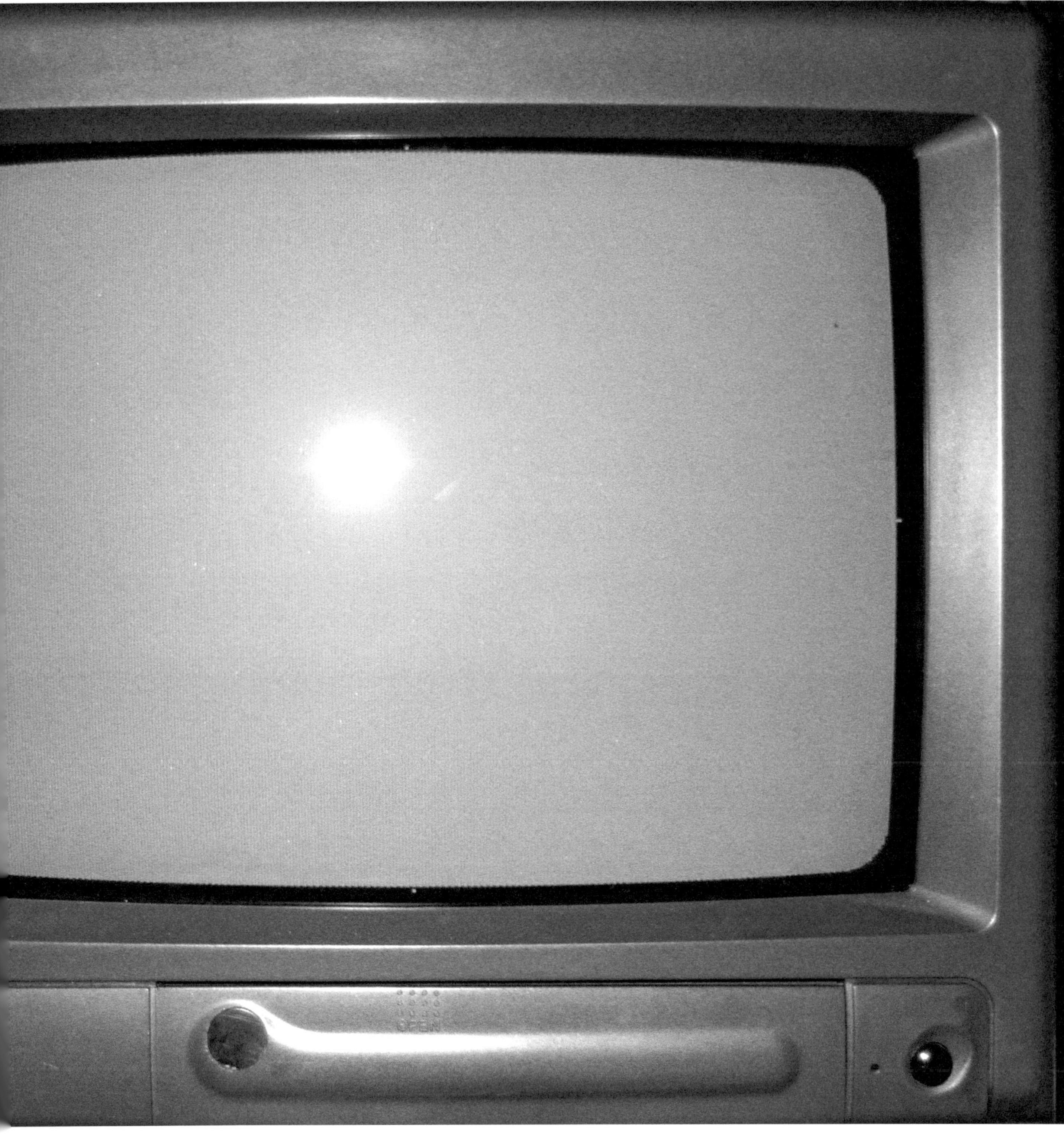
OPEN

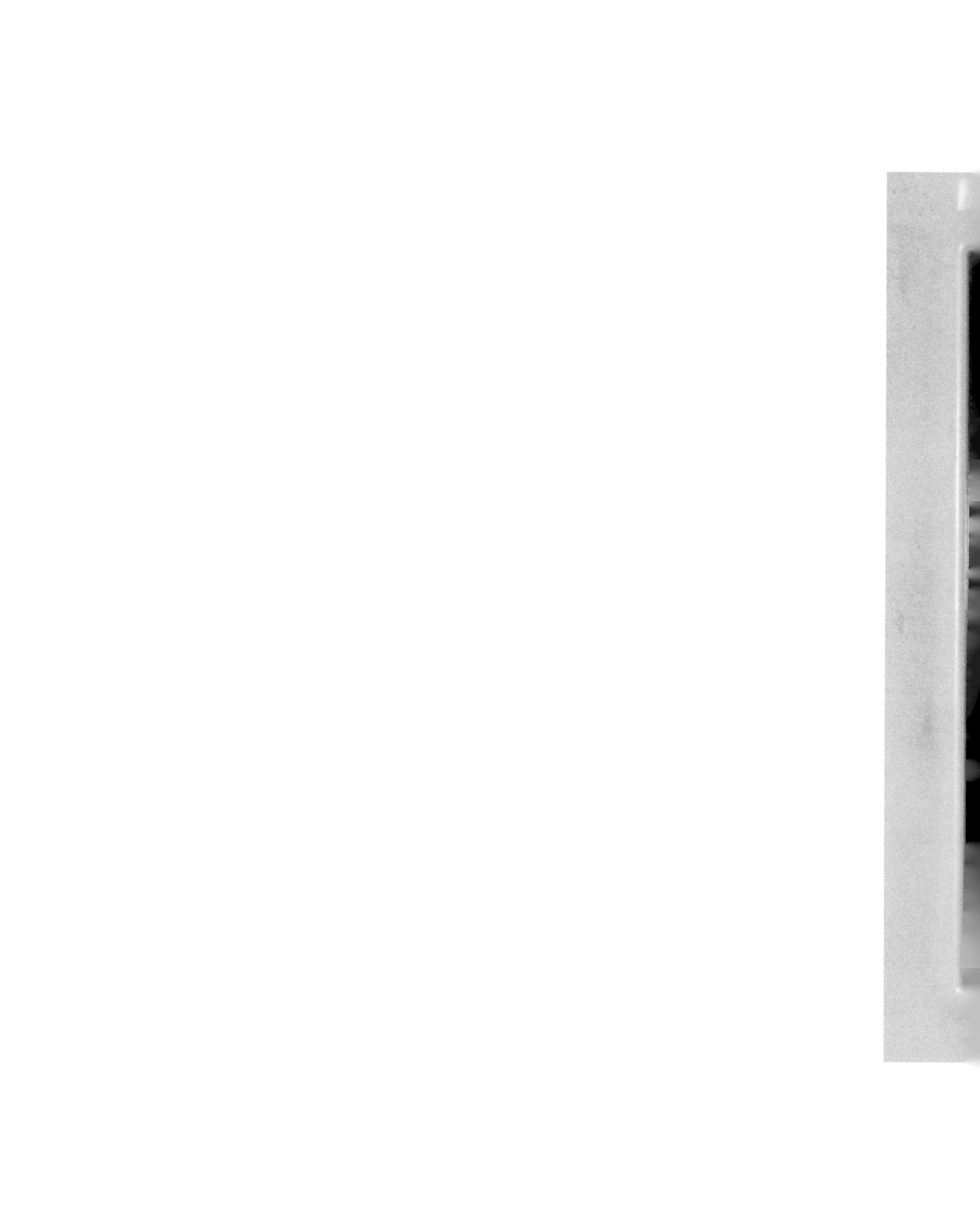

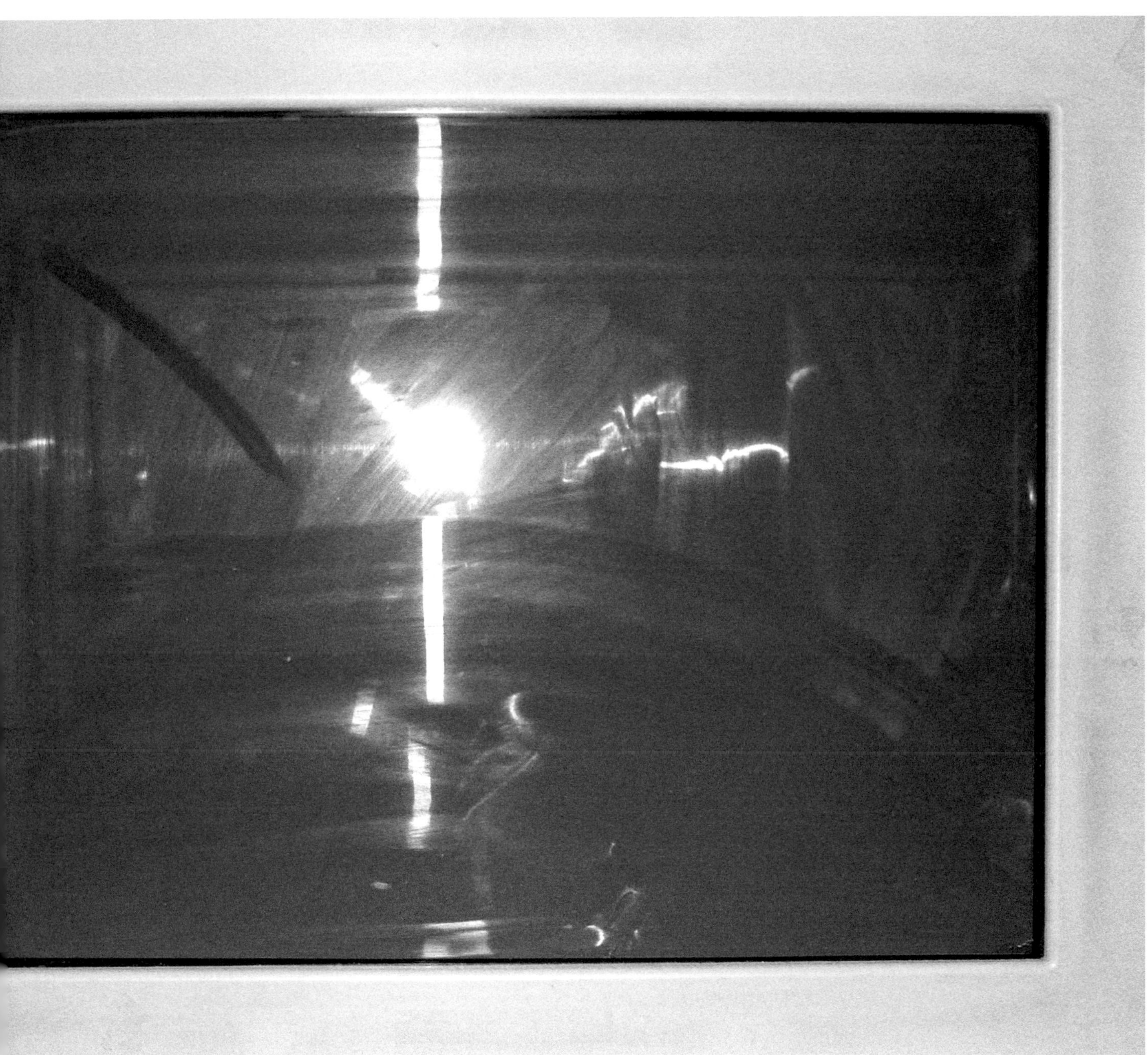

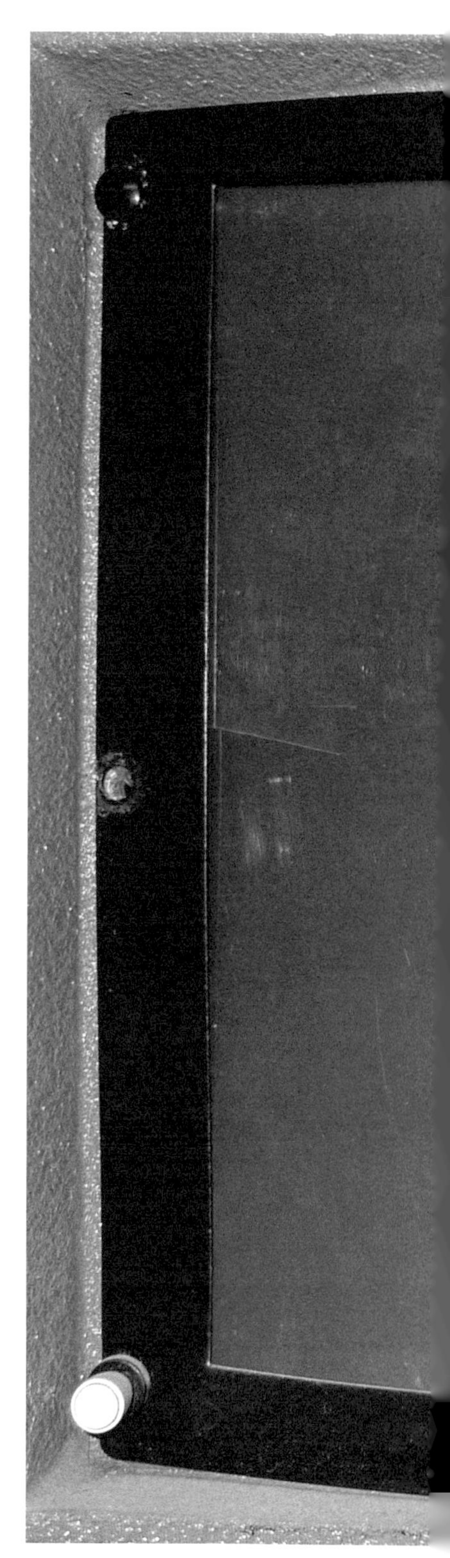

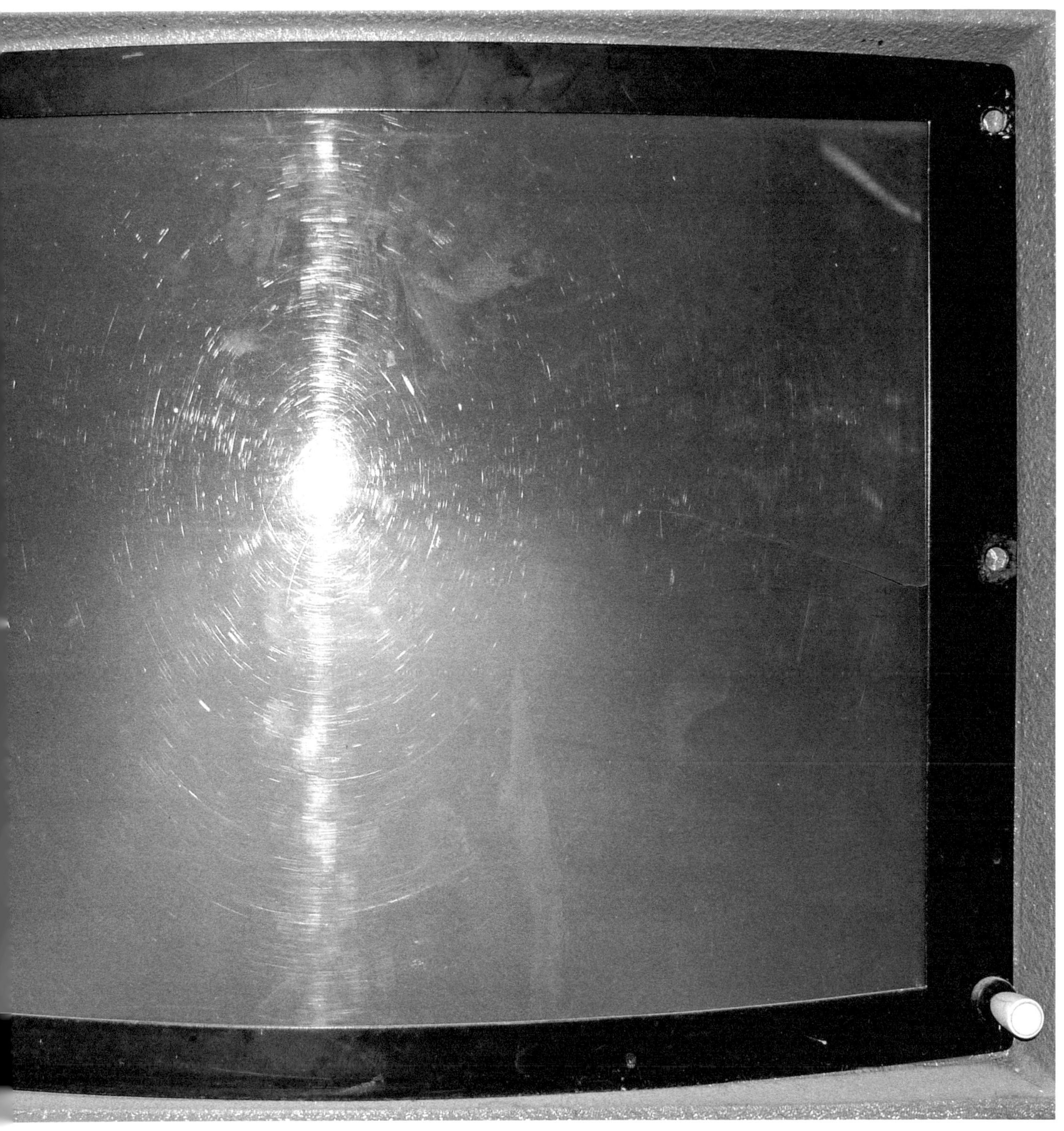

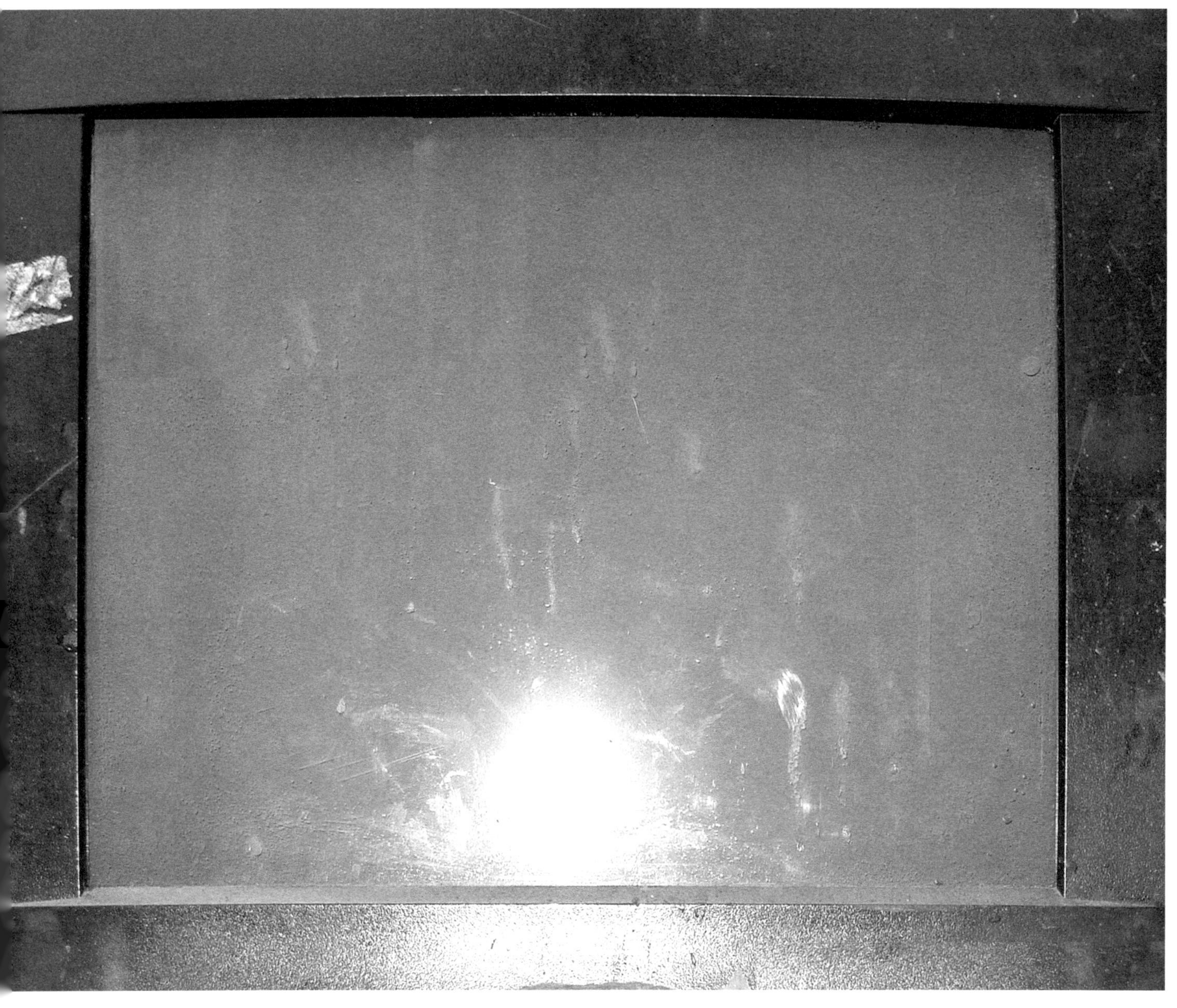

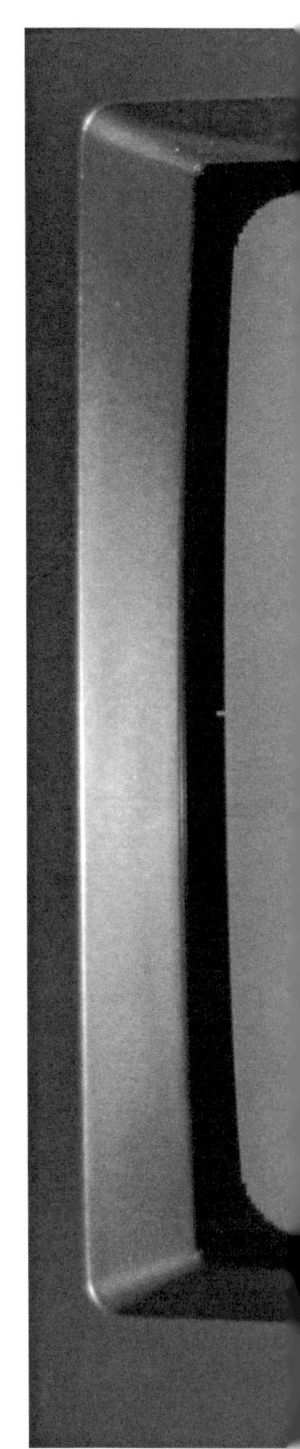

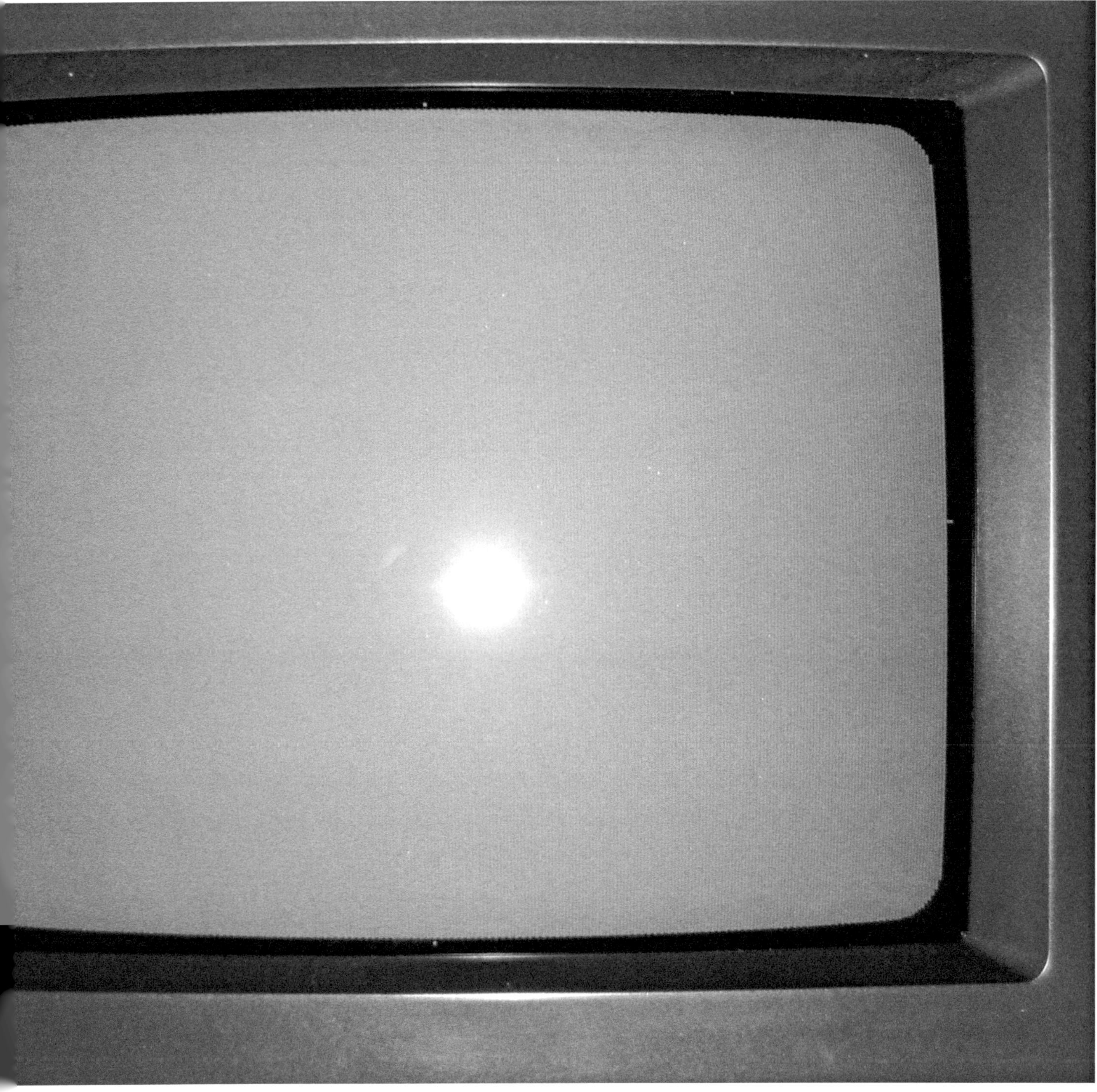

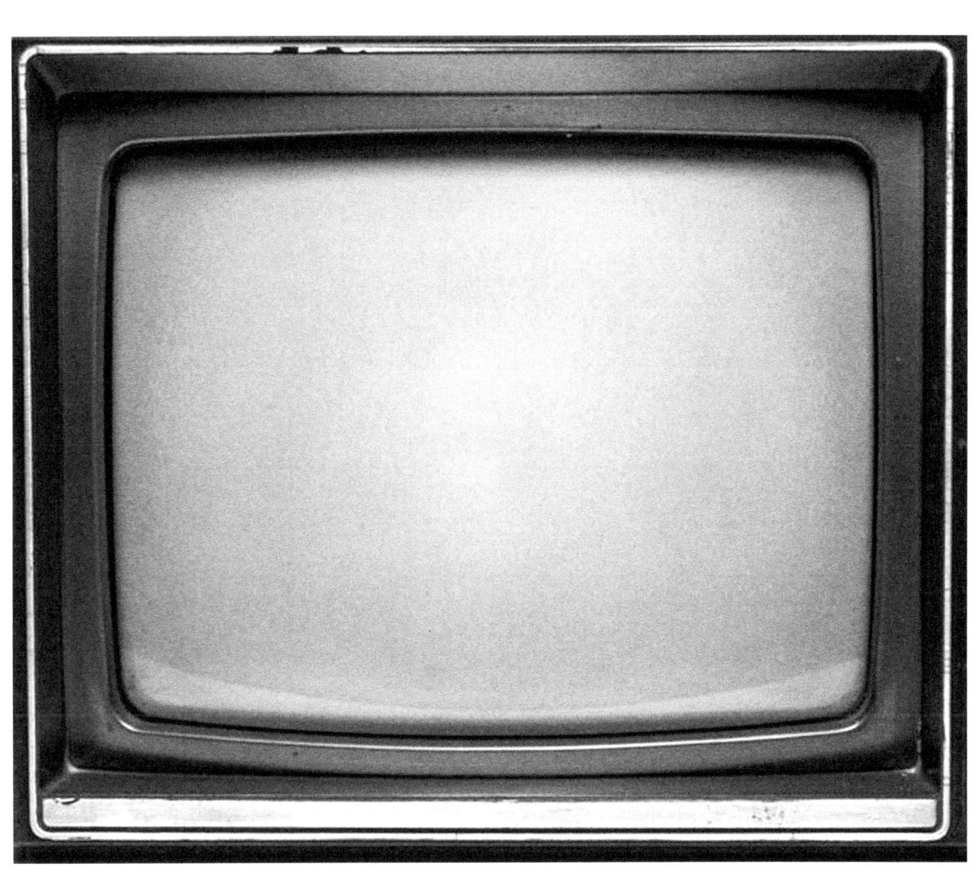

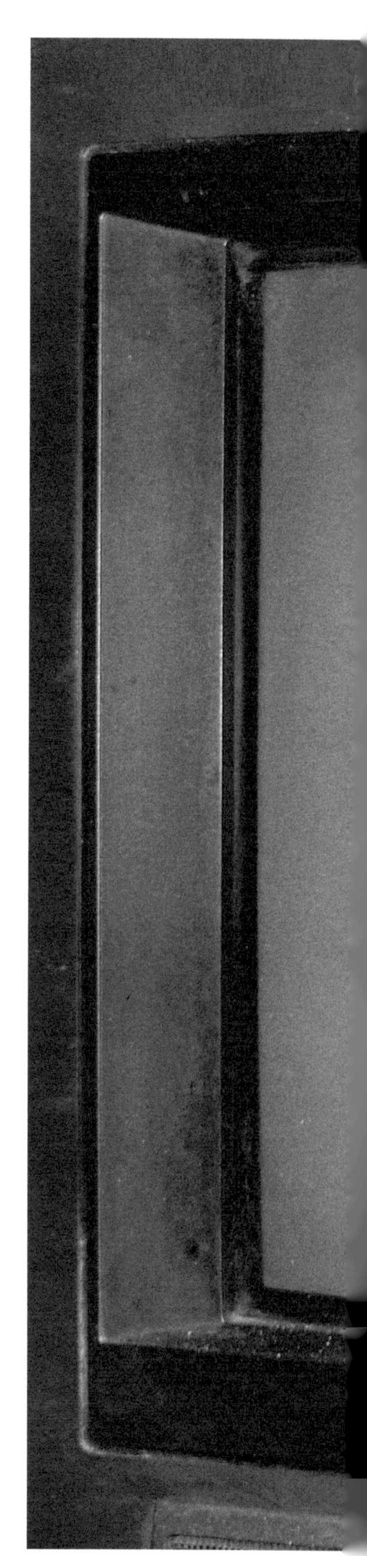

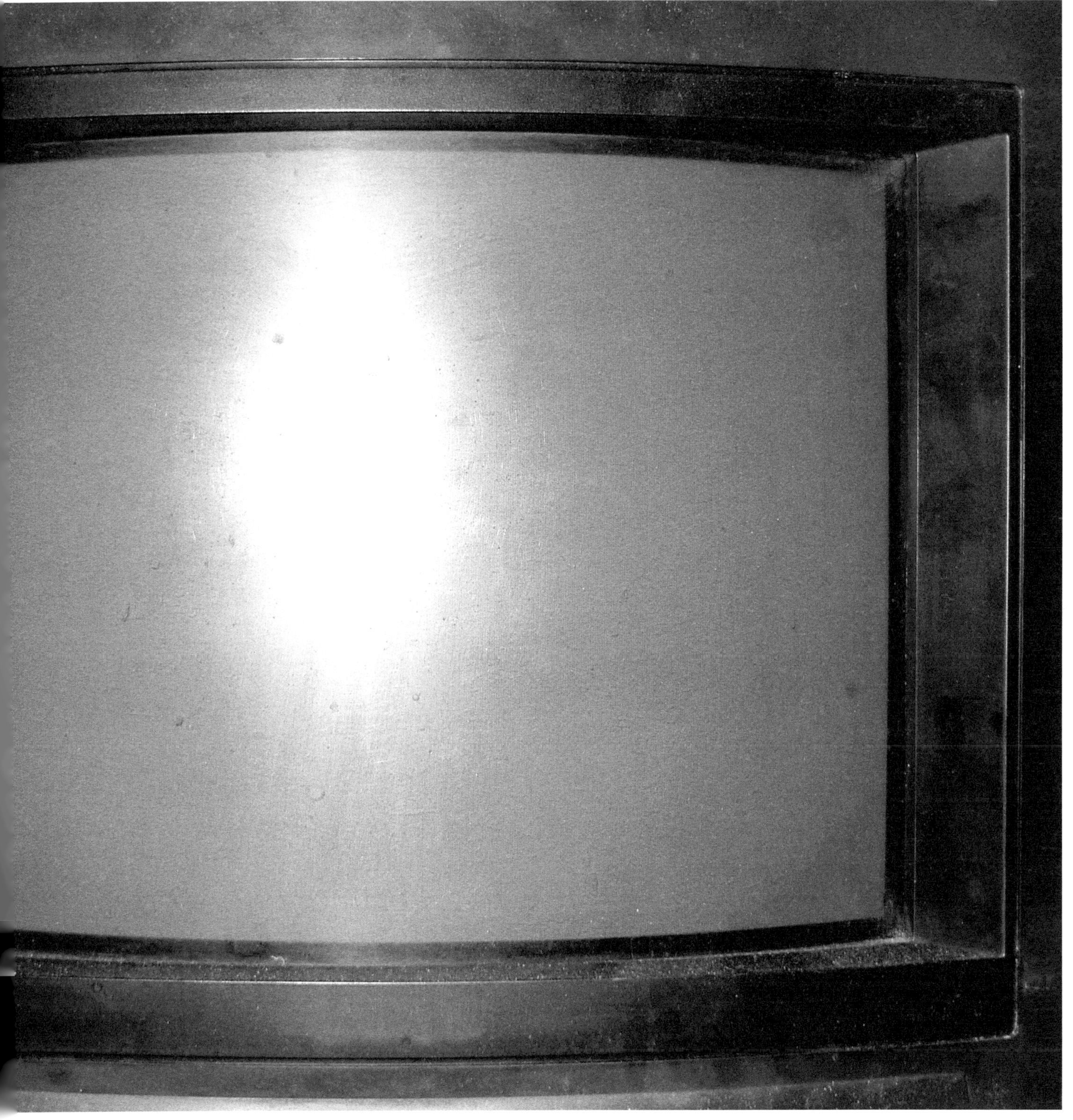

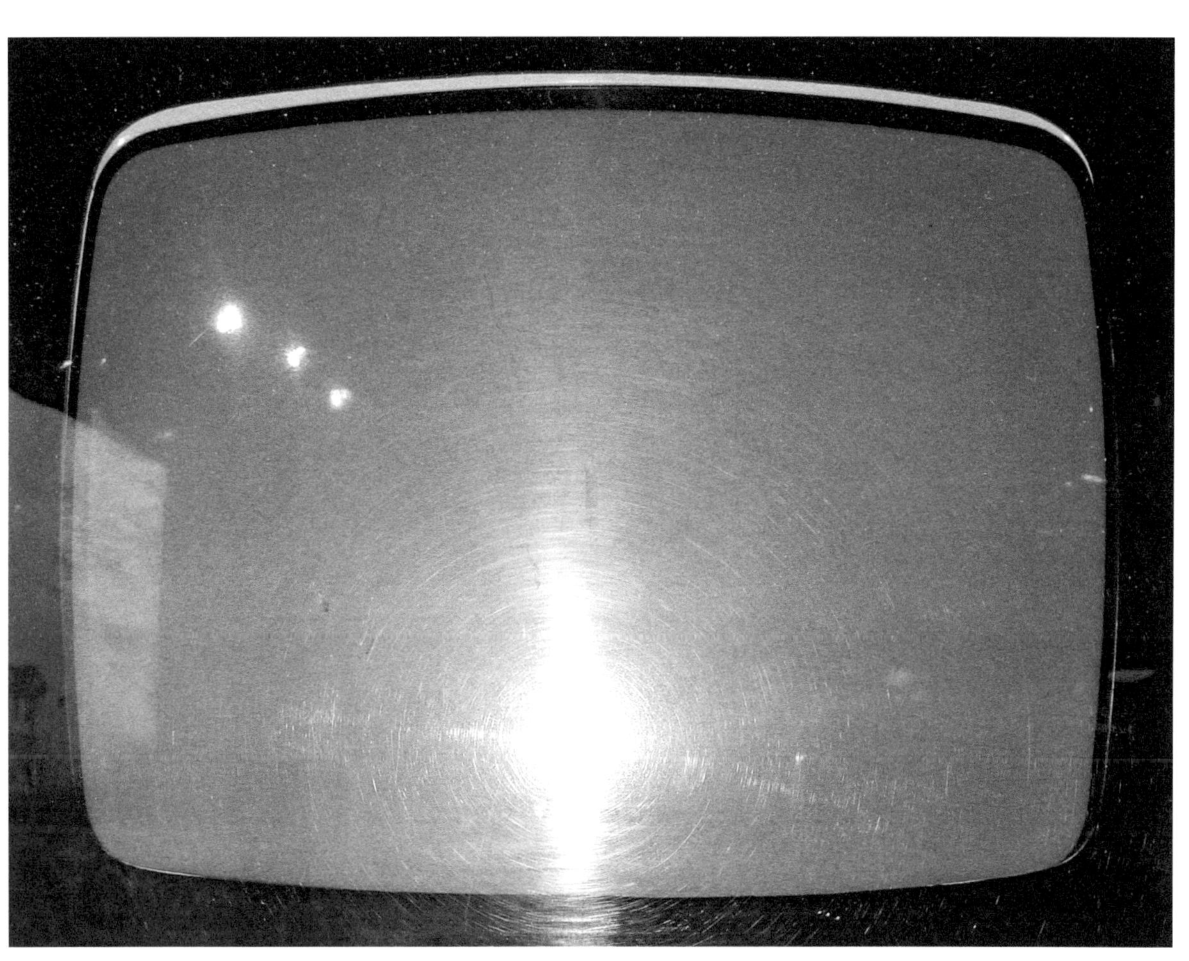

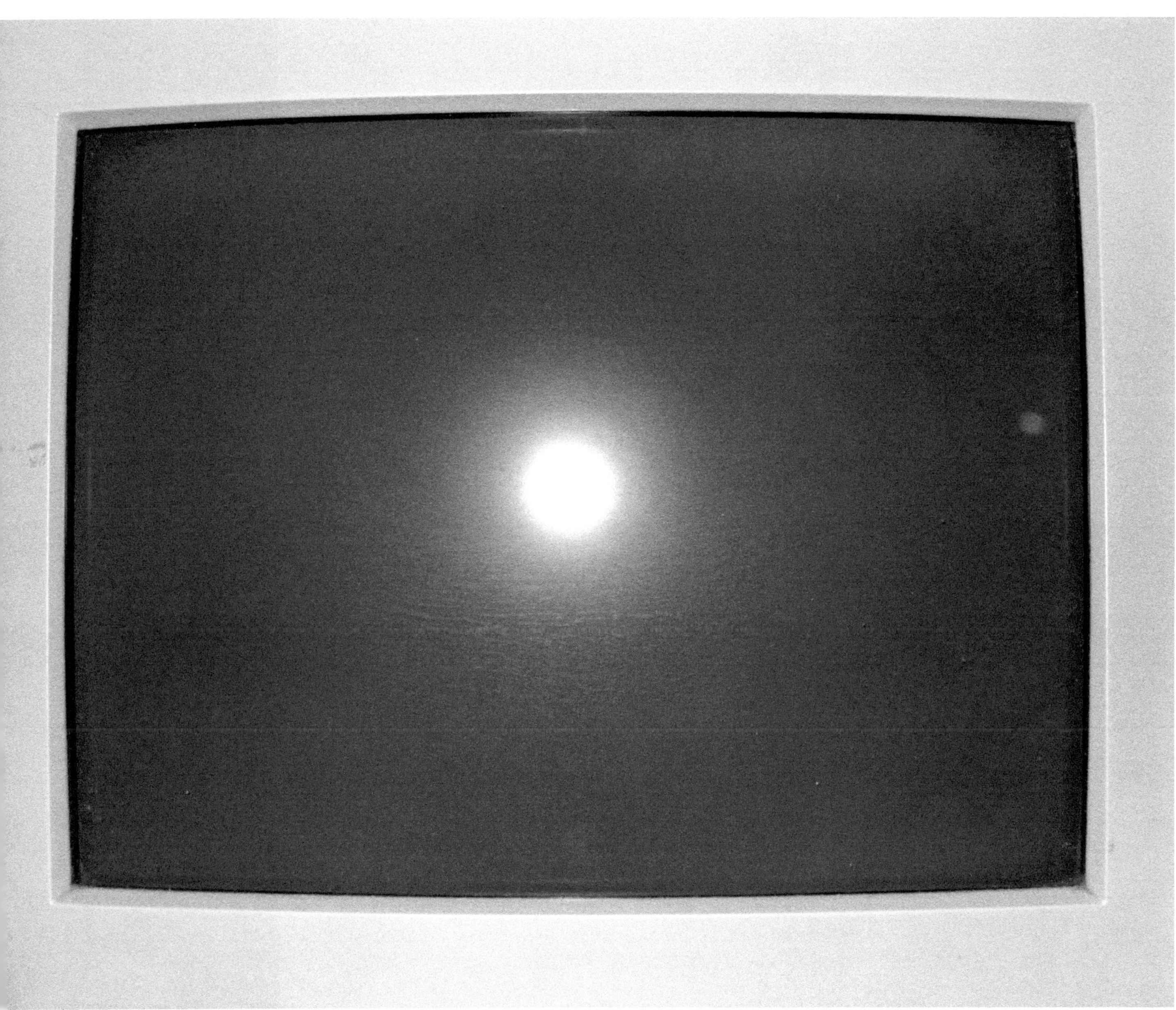

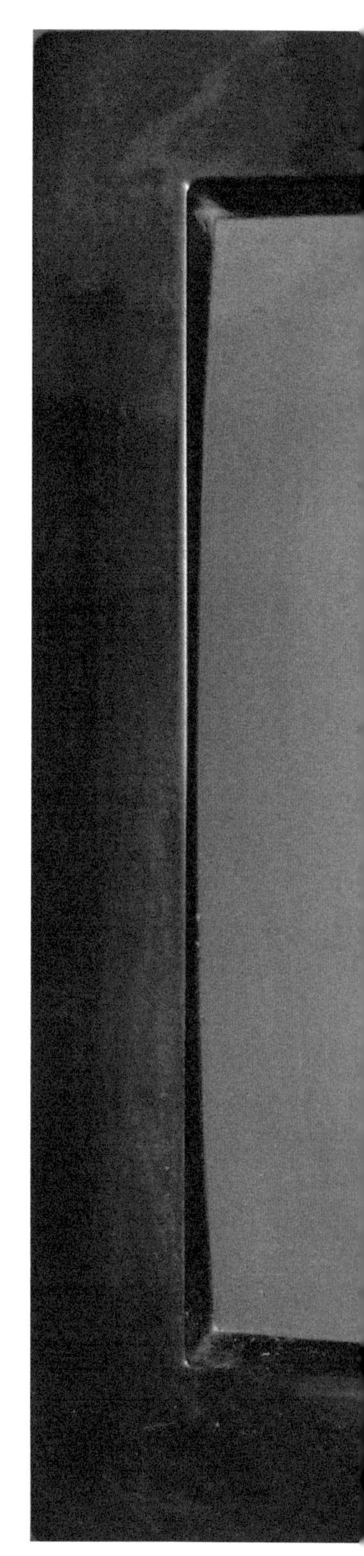

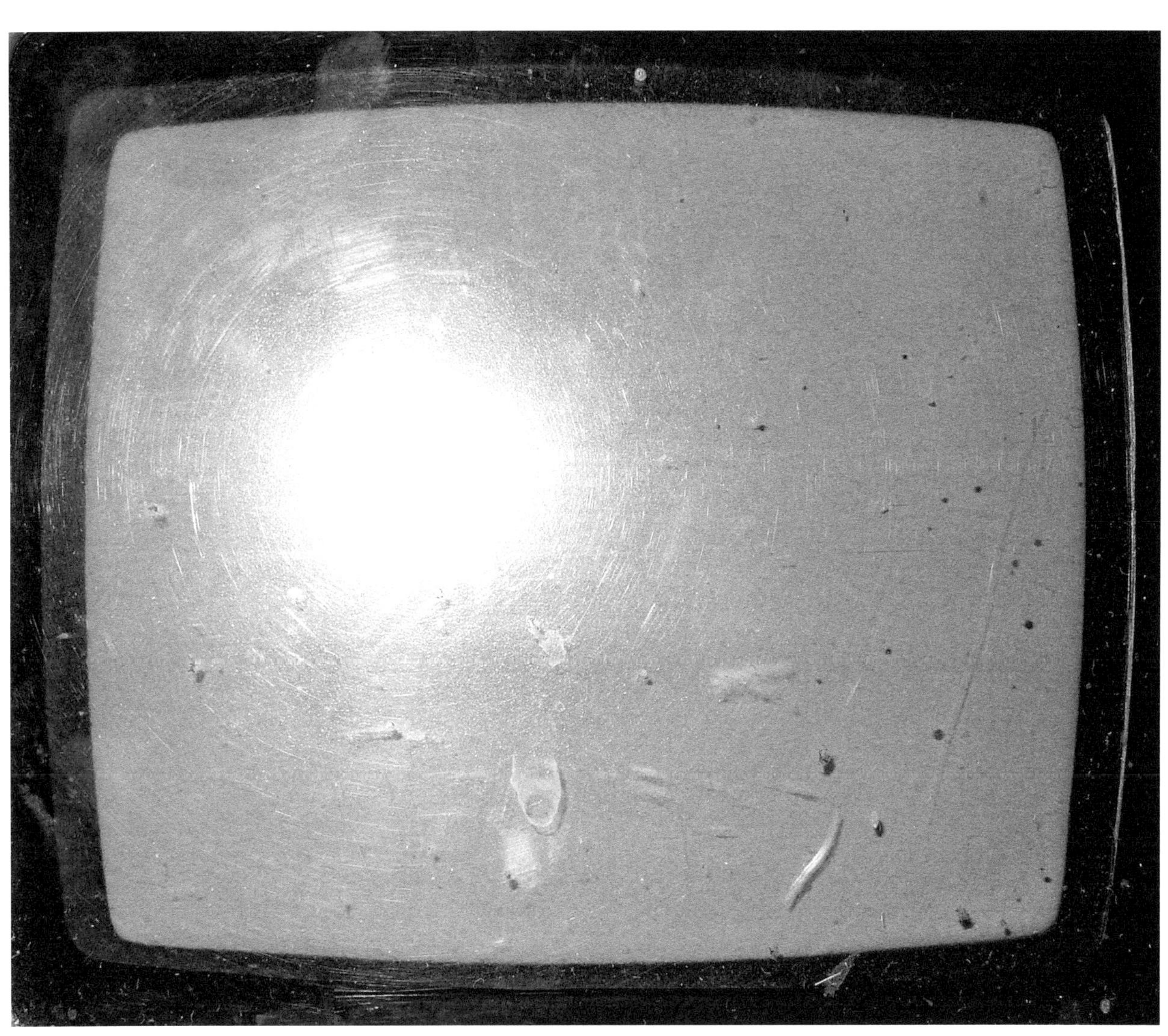

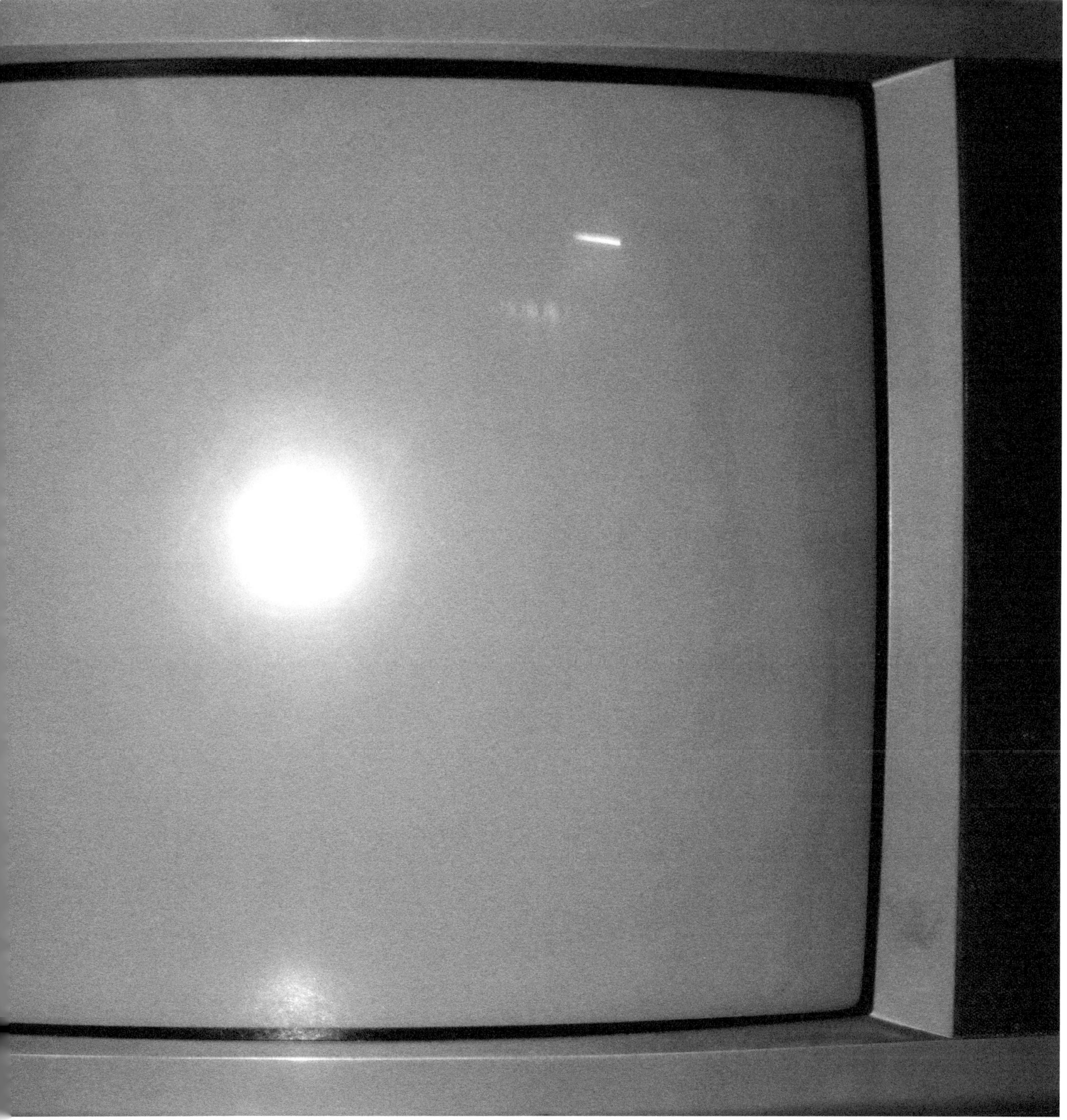

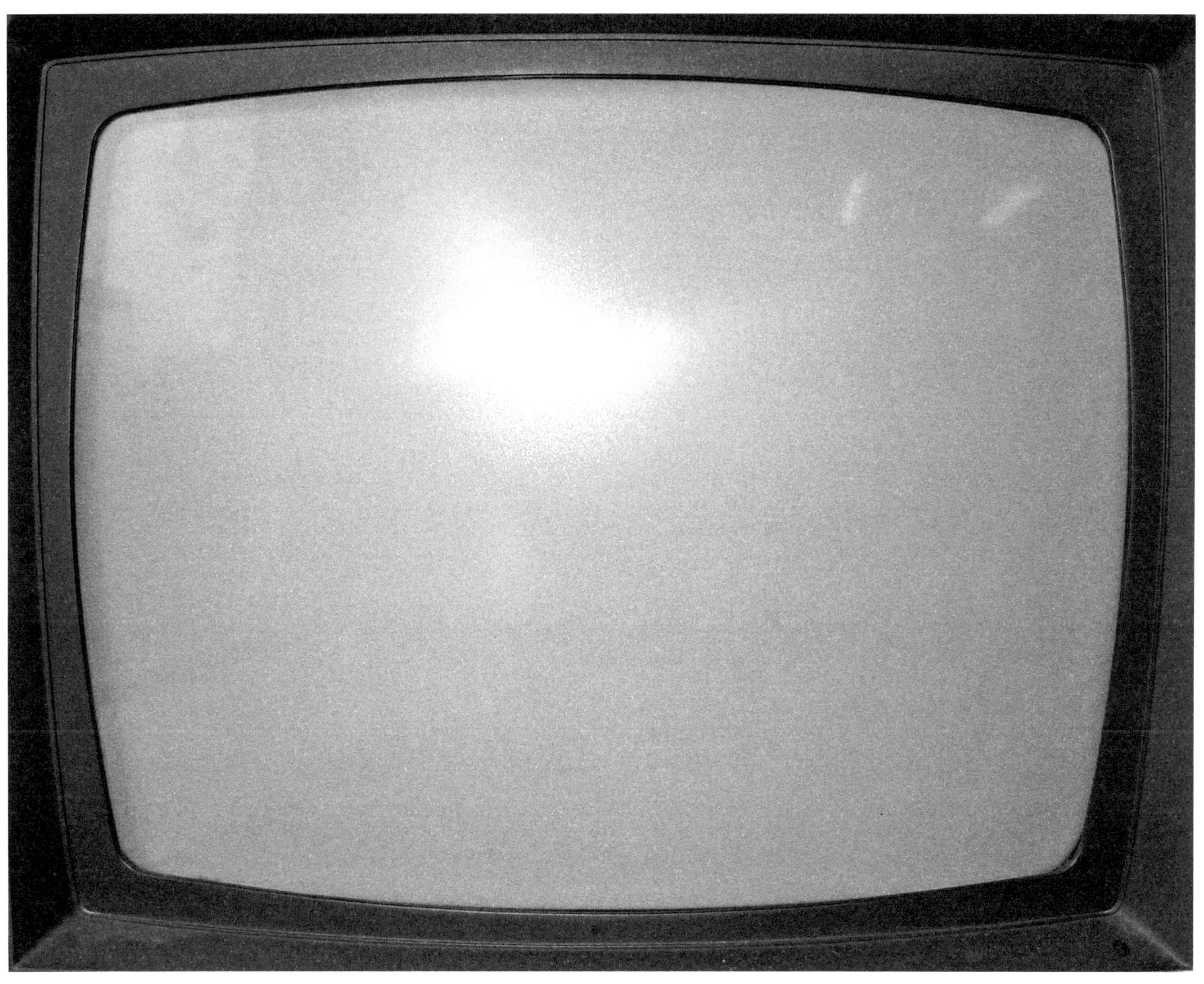

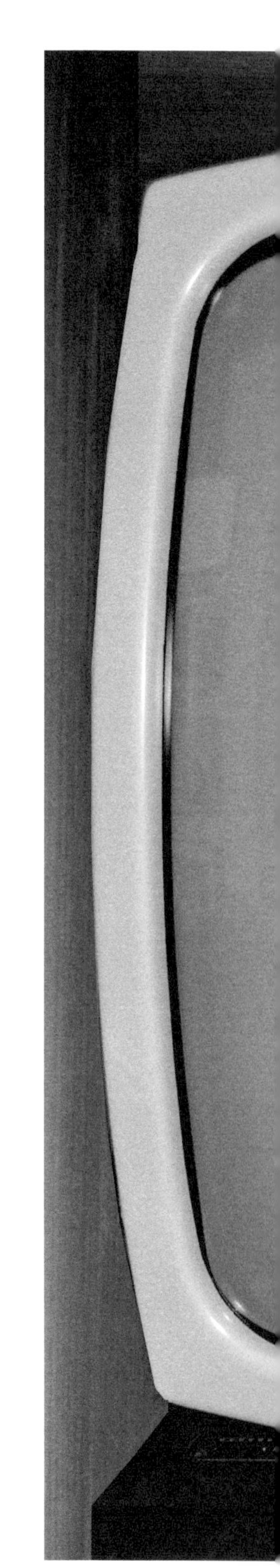

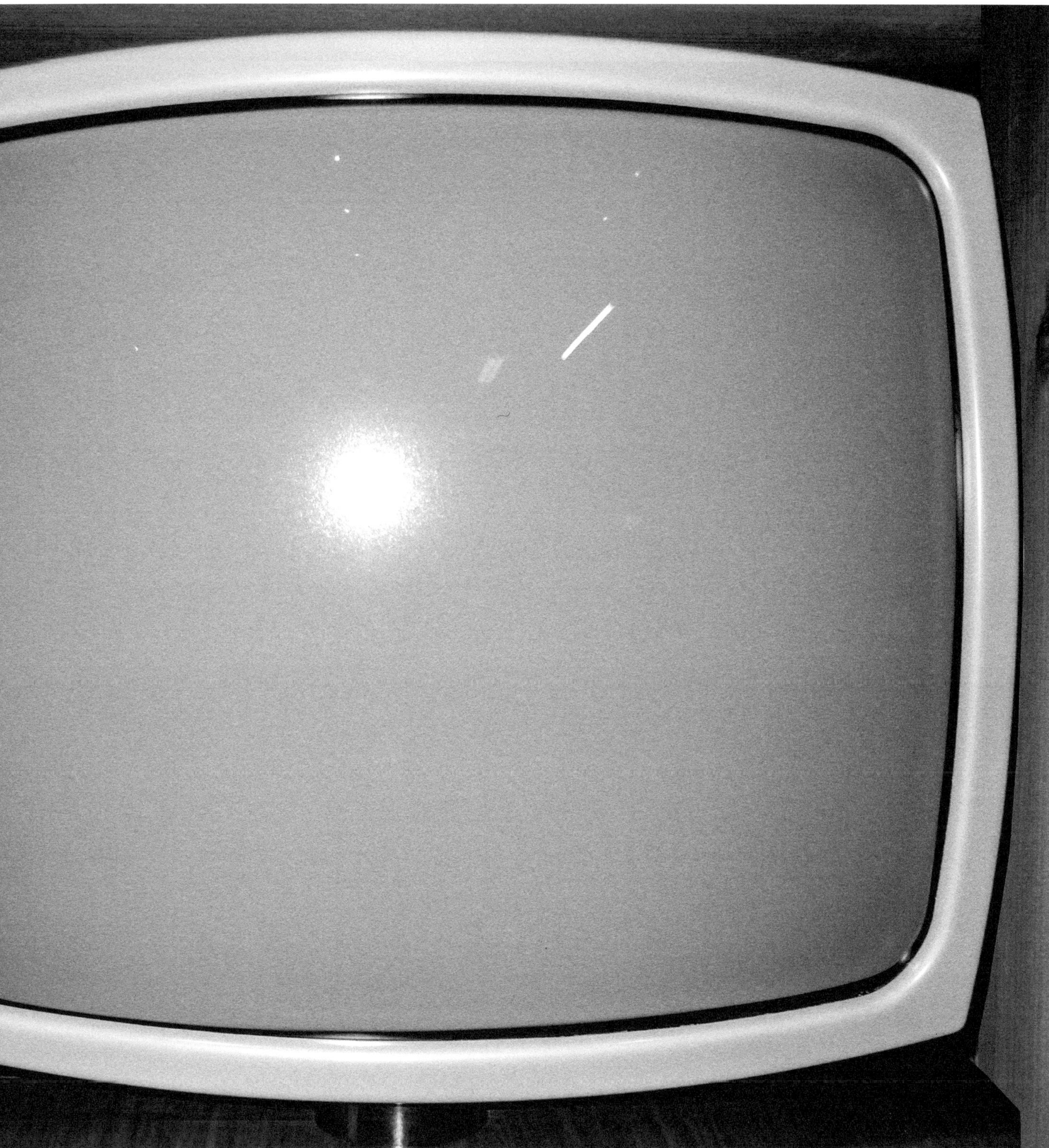

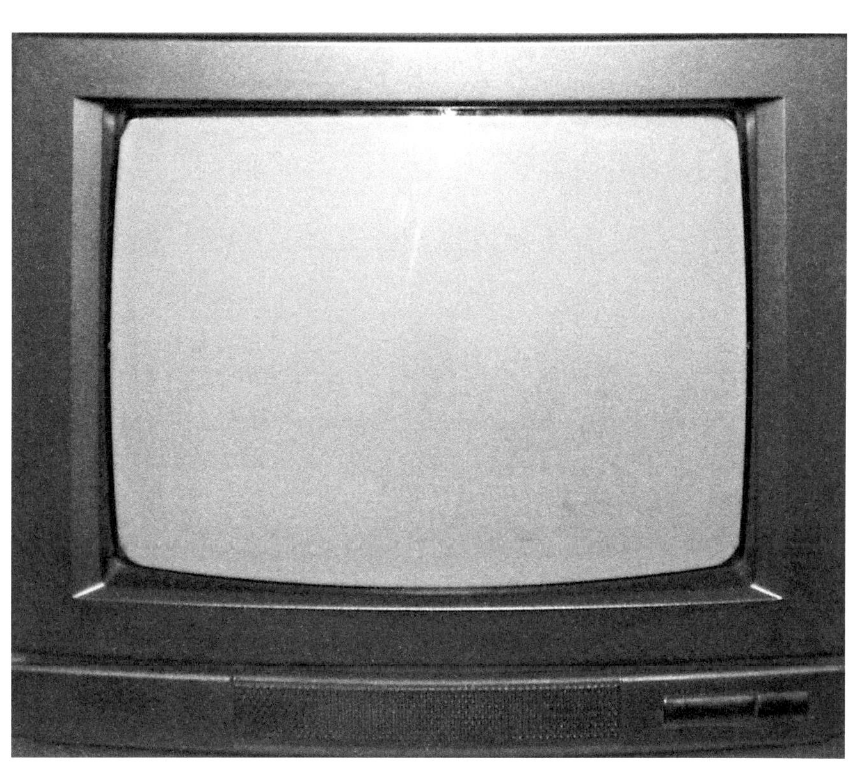

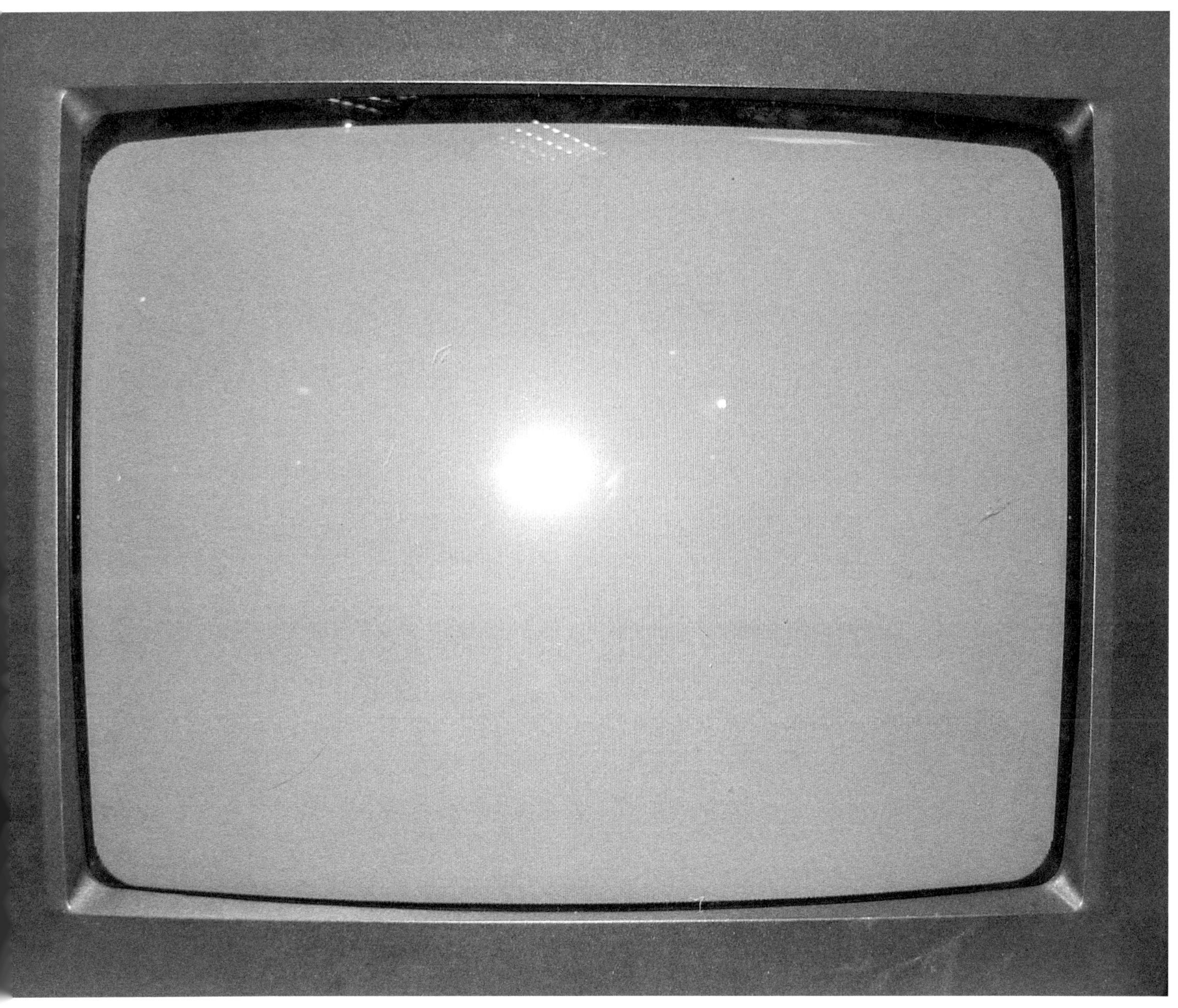

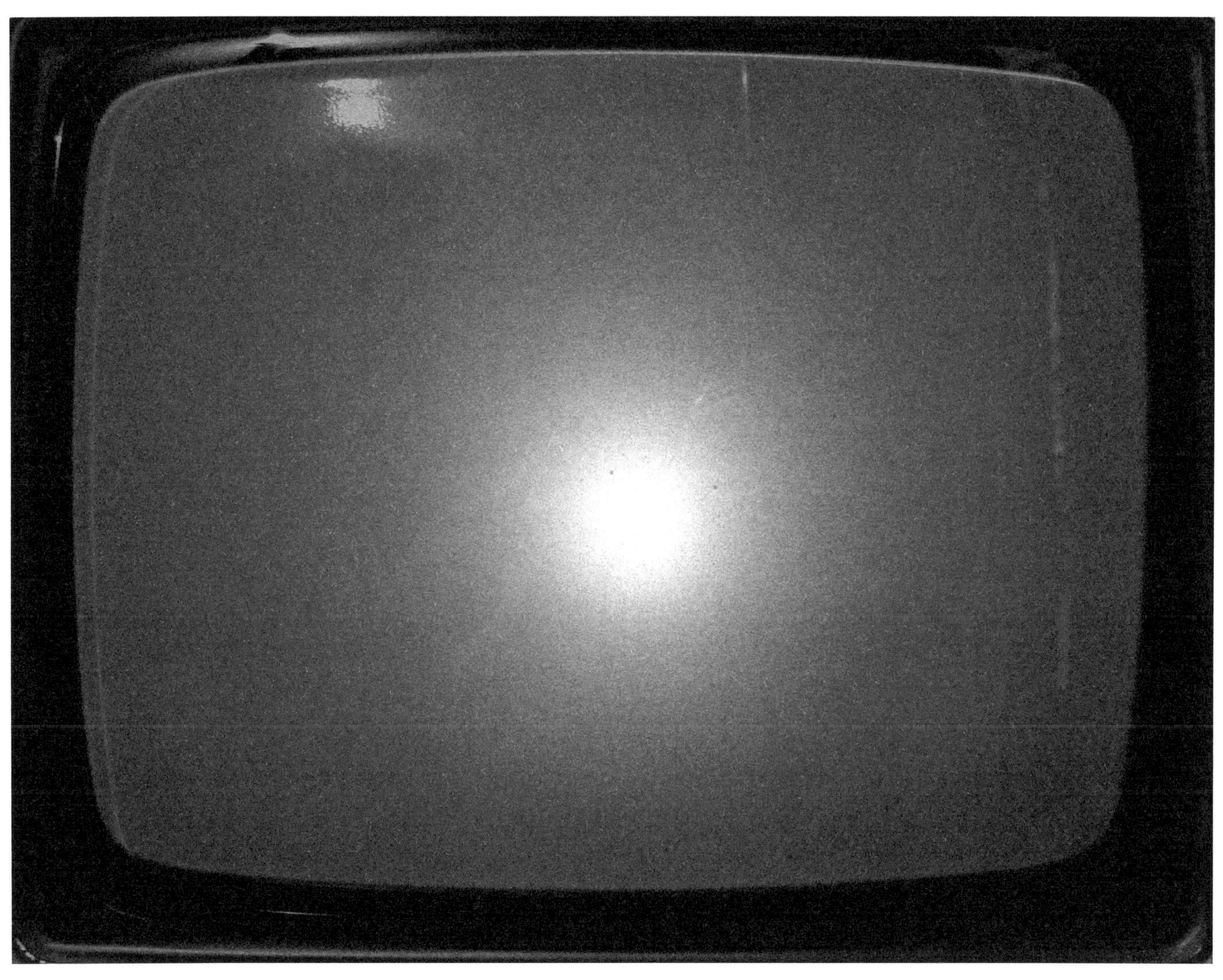

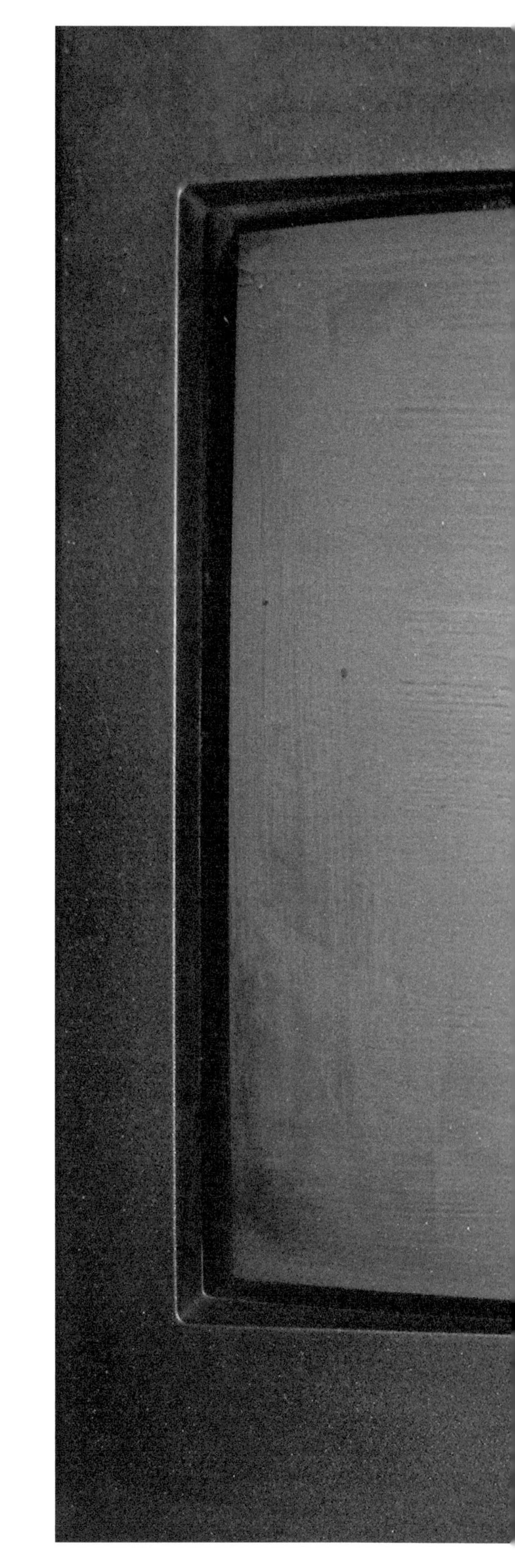

OFF

LANDSCHAFTEN MIT SONNENUNTERGANG

PAESAGGI CON TRAMONTO

LANDSCAPES WITH SUNSET

Text by Renata Stih

Die Fotoserie OFF von Daniela Comani ist ein Exkurs über Wahrnehmung in Bezug auf Medien. Mit minutiöser Präzision untersucht sie das vertraute Gerät zur Wiedergabe von laufenden Bildern im Off-Zustand: Ausgeschaltet wirken Fernseher wie tot; sie werden zu kalten Gegenständen, aber auch zu Projektionsflächen für Betrachter. Ist das Bild erloschen, ist es trotzdem kein sinnentleertes Gerät, denn die dunkle Mattscheibe reflektiert den Raum, die Personen und die Gegenstände darin.

Daniela Comani fotografiert nicht einfach nur inaktive Fernsehgeräte, sie blitzt sie: Der Flash auf der dunklen Scheibe ist wie ein Urknall, der etwas Neues entstehen lässt und gleichzeitig das Spiegelbild der Protagonistin überstrahlt und auslöscht. Dieses kurze Aufleuchten geht im Augenblick des Auslösens mit der Oberflächenstruktur der Geräte eigenwillige Verbindungen ein, es entstehen neue Bilder und neue Formen: Landschaften mit Sonnenuntergang in Kleinformat.

Daniela Comanis Fotoserie ist auch ein Exkurs über Design: Minimalistisch inszeniert sie eine Sammlung von Fernsehgeräten, verschieden in Form, Größe und Ausführung – wobei die Künstlerin die Namen der Marken akribisch entfernt hat, um das Charakteristische des Objekts in seiner Eigenheit herauszustellen. Die Objekte sind frontal fotografiert, als ob sie Personen wären, die aus dem Bild heraus die Betrachter anschauen. Das jeweilige Gehäuse des Fernsehers wirkt wie ein Bilderrahmen und betont den Bildbezug des technischen Geräts. Durch die Fotografie werden die plastischen Geräte zum zweidimensionalen Bild, das Daniela Comani dann auf eine Tafel aufzieht und so wiederum in ein dreidimensionales Objekt umwandelt. Jedes Bild ist ein Unikat, trotz des seriellen Charakters der Fotografie im Hinblick auf deren technische Reproduzierbarkeit.

La serie fotografica OFF di Daniela Comani è una digressione sulla percezione in rapporto ai media. L'artista analizza con minuziosa precisione l'apparecchio familiare per la riproduzione di immagini in movimento, l'oggetto televisore è però spento: OFF. I televisori spenti sembrano morti. Anche se l'immagine è sparita, tuttavia l'apparecchio non è privo di significato, in quanto il vetro opaco della tivù riflette in se stesso stanza, persone e oggetti.

Daniela Comani non fotografa semplicemente televisori inattivi, li fotografa con l'uso del flash. Il flash sullo schermo spento è come un big bang che crea qualcosa di nuovo e nello stesso tempo eclissa l'immagine riflessa della protagonista. Questo breve lampo, nel momento del contatto con la superficie dello schermo, scatena effetti particolari creando nuove immagini e nuove forme: paesaggi con tramonti di piccolo formato.

La serie fotografica di Daniela Comani è anche una digressione sul design: mette in scena in modo minimalista una collezione di apparecchi televisivi vecchi, di diverse forme, grandezze e modelli - per quanto l'artista abbia accuratamente cancellato i nomi delle marche, evidenziando così il carattere plastico dell'oggetto. Tali oggetti sono fotografati frontalmente, quasi fossero persone che guardano gli spettatori. La cassa del televisore fa pensare ad una cornice e sottolinea l'immagine di riferimento all'apparecchio tecnico. I televisori da oggetti plastici diventano, attraverso la fotografia, immagini bidimensionali, che Daniela Comani poi applica su un supporto di legno trasformandoli di nuovo in oggetti tridimensionali. Con questo processo di lavoro, nonostante la natura seriale della fotografia in termini della sua riproducibilità tecnica, ogni immagine diventa un pezzo unico.

OFF, a photographic series by Daniela Comani, is an excursus into perception as it relates to the media. With painstaking precision she probes that ever-present device for the reproduction of moving images, the television set, but in off mode: turned off, TV sets seem dead, they become cold objects – and yet concomitantly they serve as surfaces for viewers to project their own fantasies and fears on. Even when the picture is extinguished, the TV is not devoid of content, for the dark screen reflects the room and the people and objects in it.

Daniela Comani doesn't merely take pictures of inactive TV sets, she shoots them with flash: the flash hits the dark screen like a Big Bang that creates something new, while eclipsing the protagonist's reflection. At the split second in which the flash hits the surface of the screen, it produces peculiar effects, creating new images and shapes: small-scale landscapes with sunset.

Daniela Comani's series is also about design: for this minimalistic mise-en-scène of an assortment of TV sets of varying shape, size and design, the artist has painstakingly removed the brand names in order to bring out the physical idiosyncrasies of each different object. The objects are portrayed from the front, as though they were people gazing out from the picture at the viewer. The housing of each set serves as a picture frame and suggests this technical device's essential nexus to pictures. The photograph turns the three-dimensional TV sets into two-dimensional pictures, which Comani then mounts on wood panel to create a new three-dimensional object. As a result, despite the serial nature of photography with its technical capability of infinite reproduction, each picture becomes unique.

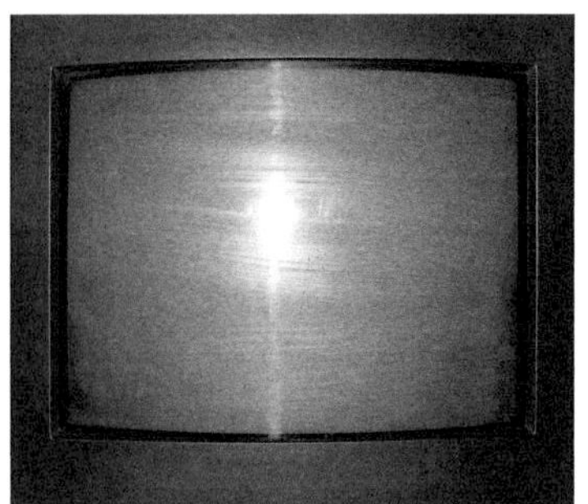
OFF #01, 60 x 70 cm

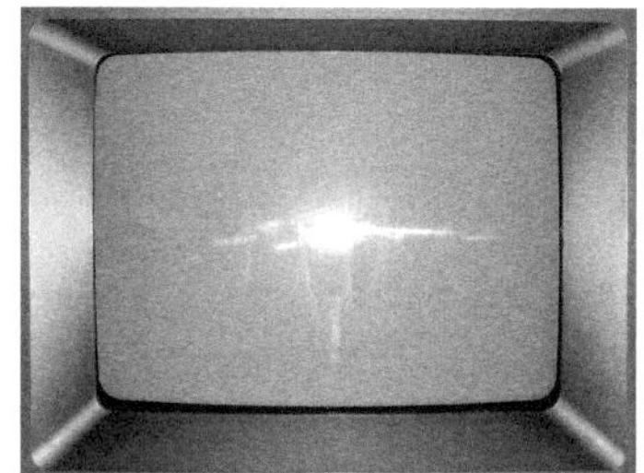
OFF #02, 52 x 70 cm

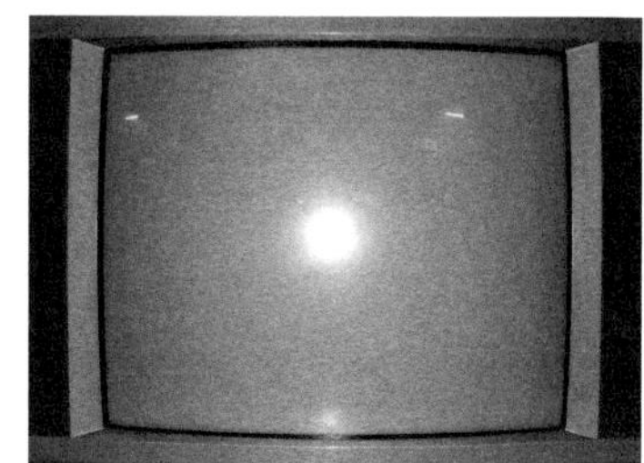
OFF #03, 50 x 70 cm

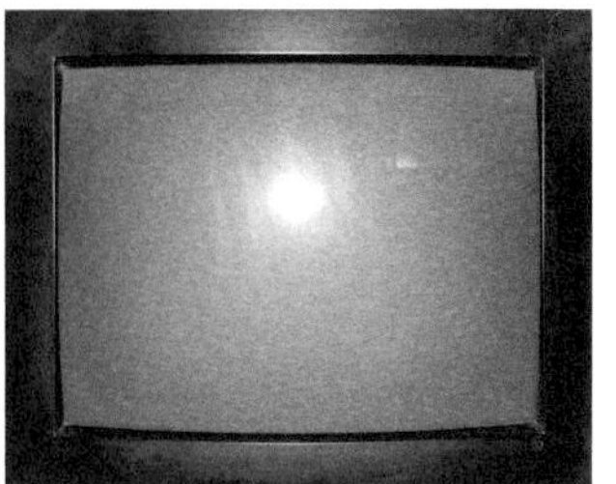
OFF #07, 50 x 61,5 cm

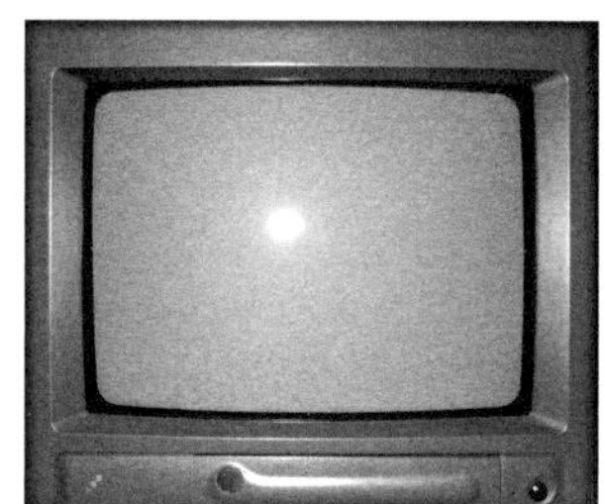
OFF #08, 50 x 60 cm

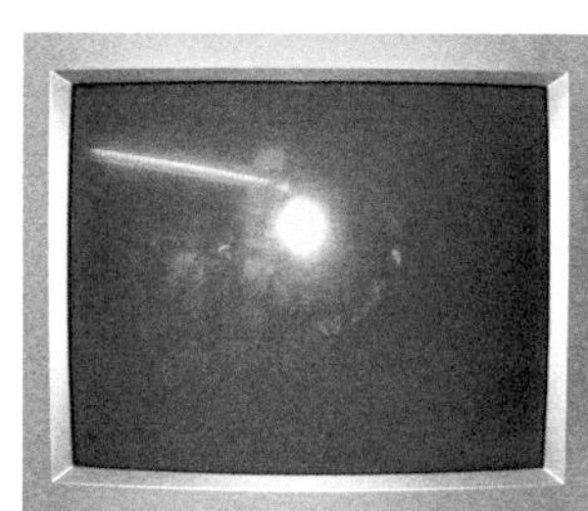
OFF #09, 50 x 60 cm

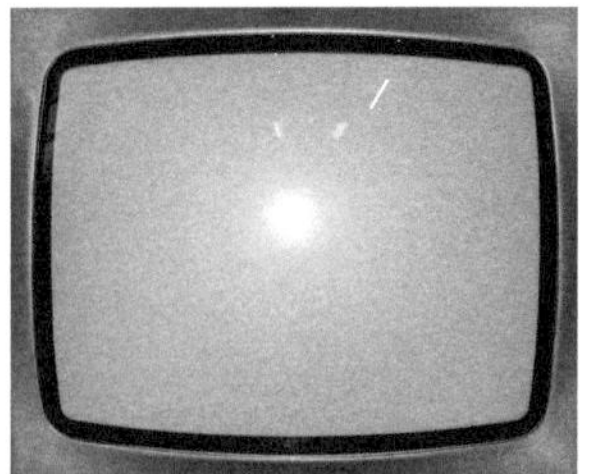
OFF #13, 47 x 58 cm

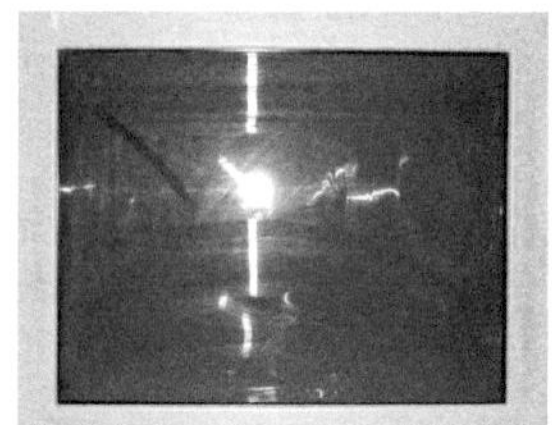
OFF #14, 43 x 58 cm

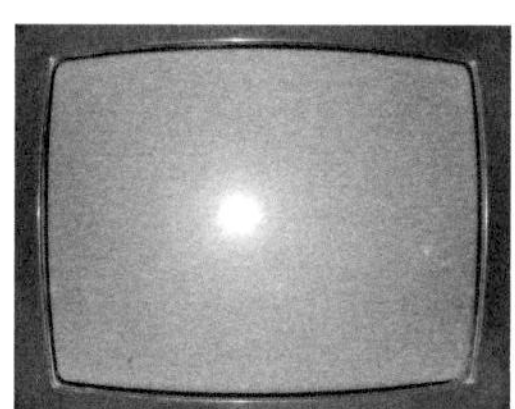
OFF #15, 40 x 52 cm

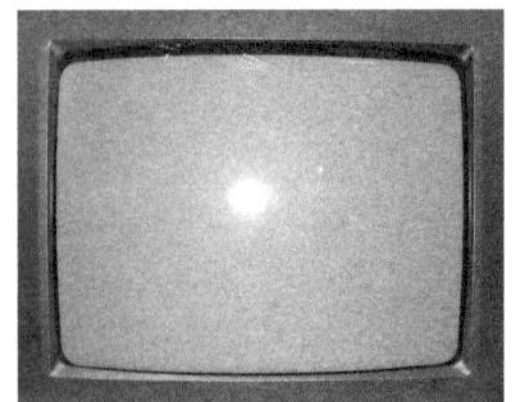
OFF #19, 40 x 50 cm

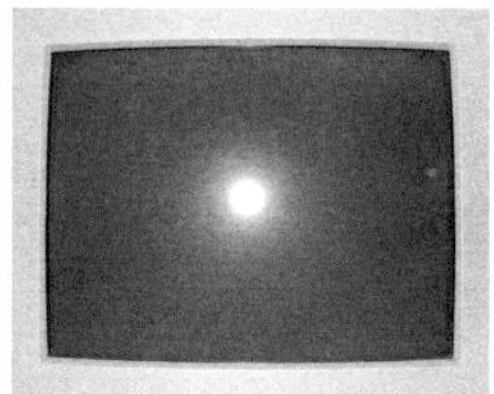
OFF #20, 40 x 50 cm

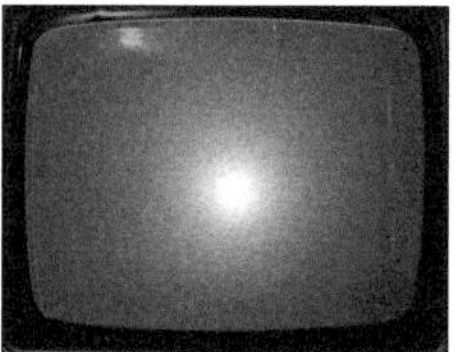
OFF #21, 35 x 46 cm

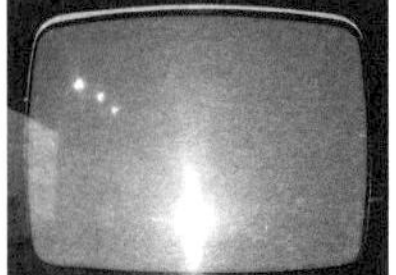
OFF #25, 30 x 40 cm

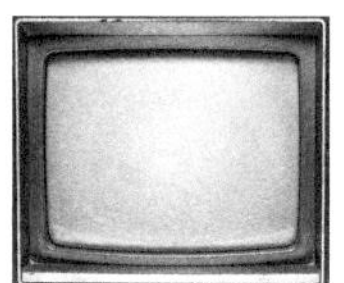
OFF #26, 27,5 x 33 cm

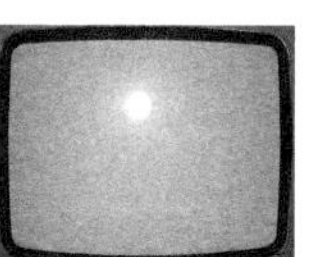
OFF #27, 24 x 30,5 cm

OFF – LANDSCAPES WITH SUNSET IS A 28-PART SERIES OF PHOTOGRAPHS (PRINTS ON ARCHIVAL PAPER, LAMINATED ON MDF) TAKEN BY DANIELA COMANI IN 2010.

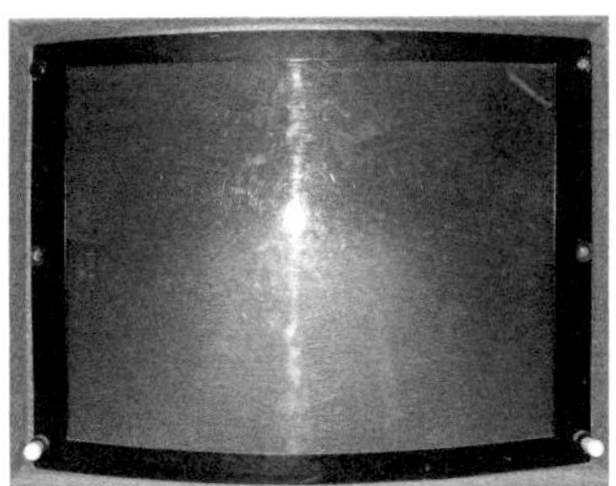
OFF #04, 50 x 65 cm

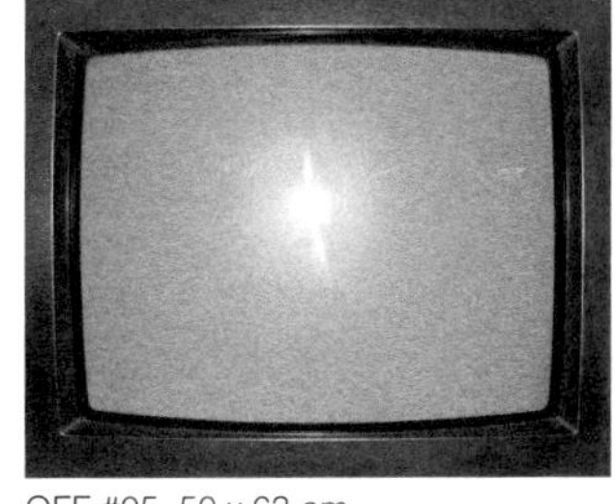
OFF #05, 50 x 63 cm

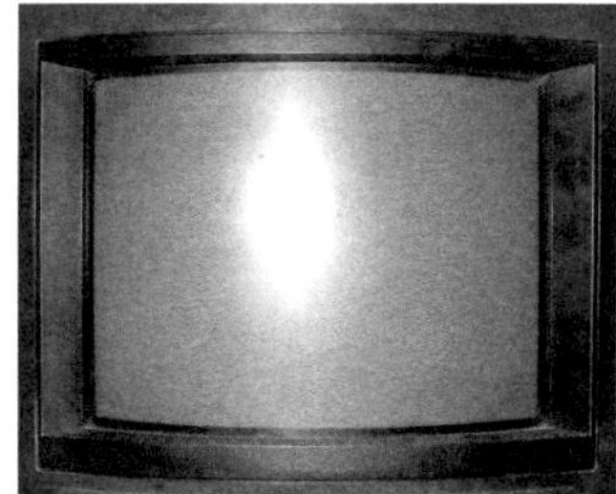
OFF #06, 50 x 62 cm

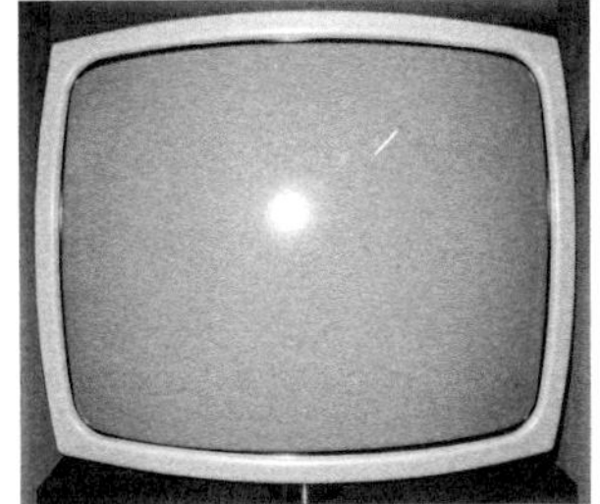
OFF #10, 51 x 59 cm

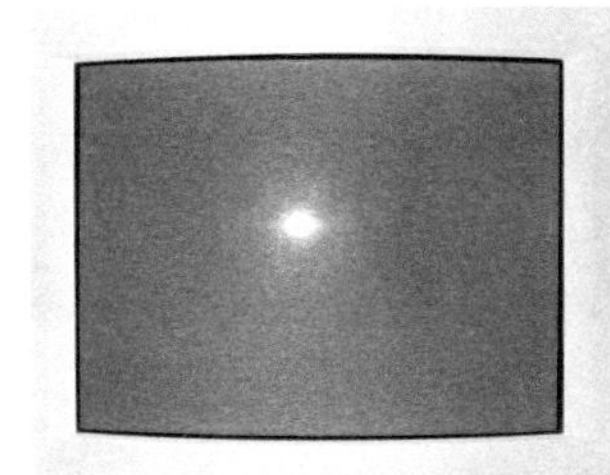
OFF #11, 48 x 60 cm

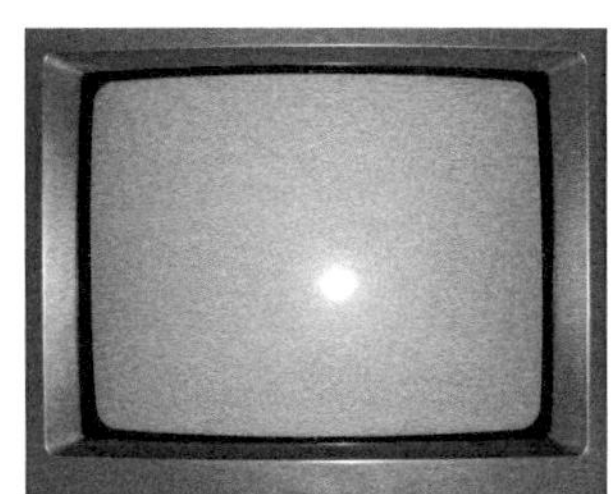
OFF #12, 47 x 59 cm

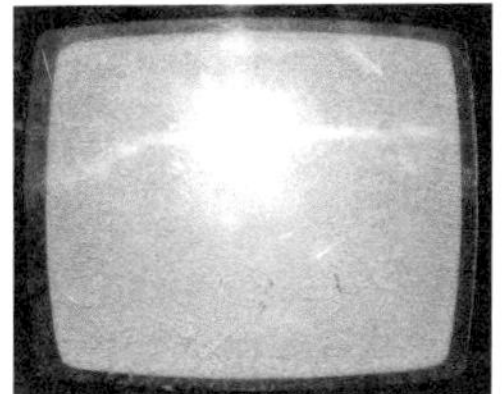
OFF #16, 40 x 50 cm

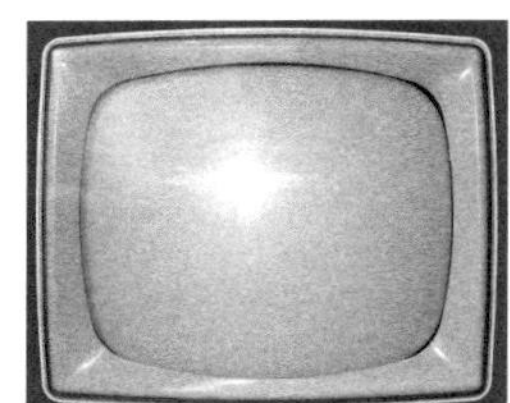
OFF #17, 40 x 50 cm

OFF #18, 40 x 50 cm

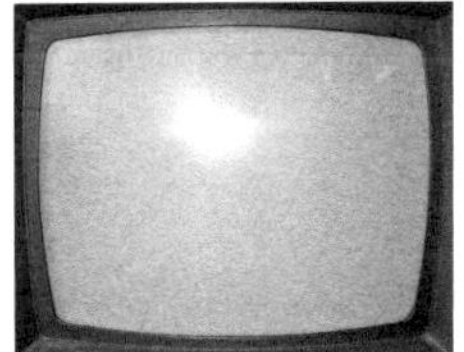
OFF #22, 35,5 X 45,5 cm

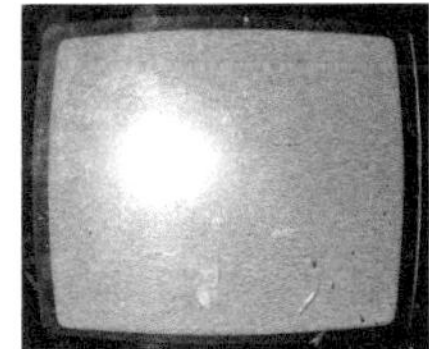
OFF #23, 35 x 42 cm

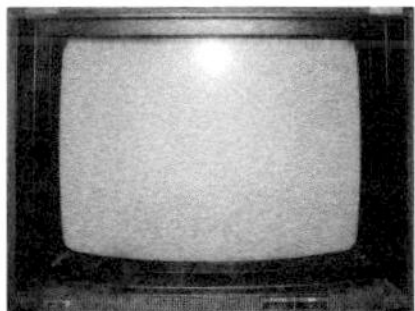
OFF #24, 31 x 42 cm

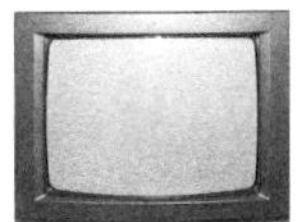
OFF #28, 24 x 28,5 cm

W BROUGHT TOGETHER IN A SINGLE BOOK, THE PRINTS ARE SCALED DOWN FOR THIS PUBLICATION TO 1:2.5 OF THEIR ORIGINAL SIZE. SCALE ON THIS PAGE: 1:15.

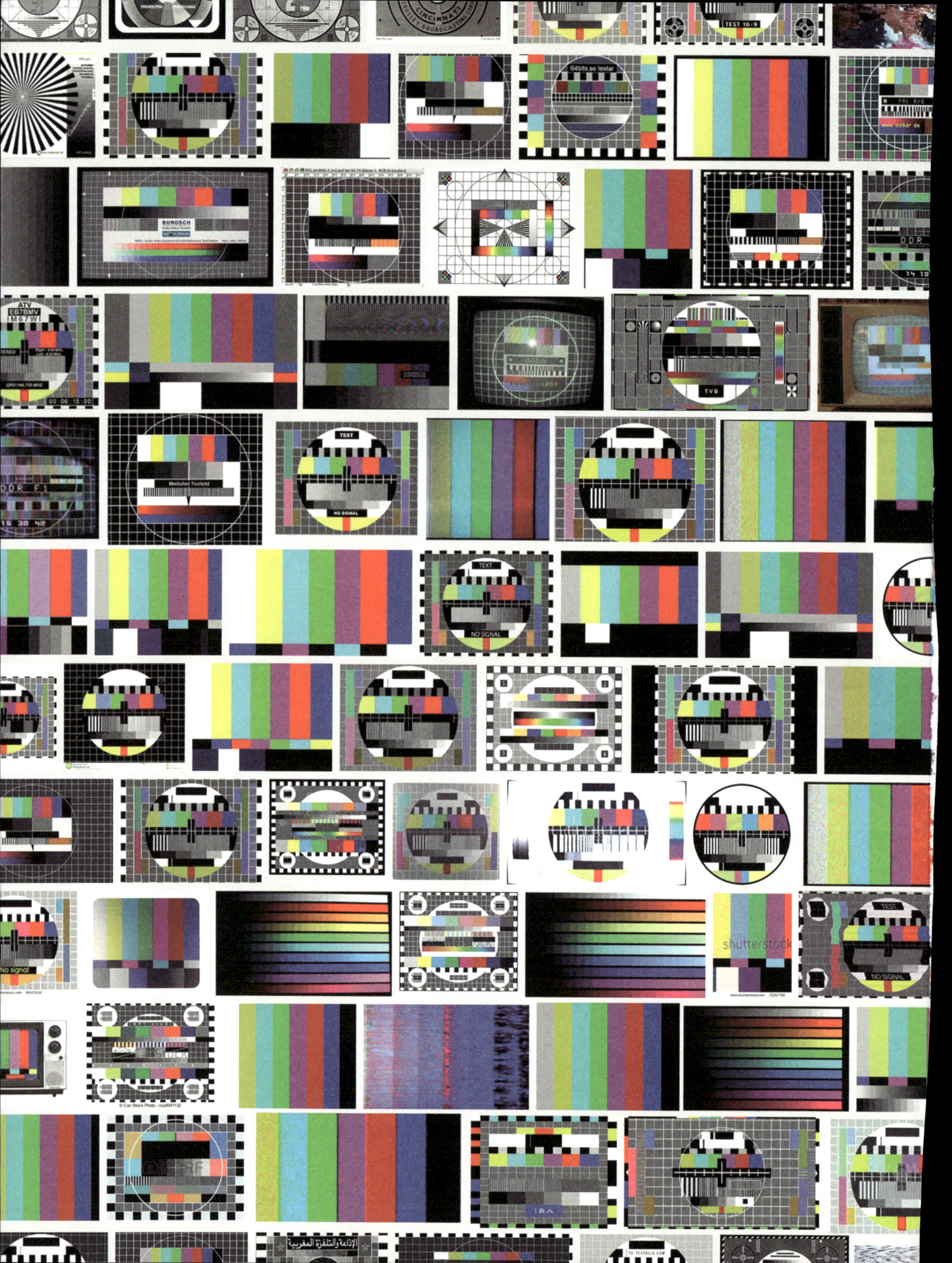

CINCINNATI
TEST 16:9
64bits.se testar
PAL B/G
www.dd8dr.de
BUROSCH
DDR
ATV
EB7BMV
TV8
TEST
NO SIGNAL
MediaNet Testbild
DDR F1
TEXT
NO SIGNAL
No signal
shutterstock
TEST
NO SIGNAL
IBA
الإذاعة والتلفزة المغربية